Praise for Divergent Church

"In a time of religious unbundling and remixing, this book tells the inspiring story of leaders and communities carrying the best of their tradition forward without demanding a denominational identity. These communities offer their gifts of vision and integrity in a culture hungry for deep connection and spiritual formation. A must-read for anyone thinking about the future of religion."
—Casper ter Kuile, Ministry Innovation Fellow, Harvard Divinity School

"We are witnessing the rise of new life forms in the taxonomy of the Western church. The first life form was house church, but by the third century the congregation became the dominant model for the next seventeen hundred years, until now. As we move from church-as-institution to church-as-movement (a necessary adjustment to position the church for relevance) we are seeing an expanded bandwidth of how church expresses itself. Tim and Kara have done us a favor to help us understand some of what is happening, especially in decoding what is 'common' in 'divergence.'"
—Reggie McNeal, best-selling author and missional leadership specialist

"Tim Shapiro and Kara Faris give us remarkable insights about the amazing new 'radically contextual' and 'church plus' faith communities they describe as divergent churches. This book is essential reading for all of us who are committed to serve both the institutional church in the midst of a major 'reformation' and the gifted new leaders and evolving new world of radically different faith communities that are continuing to accomplish God's dreams for this world."
—Tom Locke, President, Texas Methodist Foundation

"*Divergent Church* is a beautiful and hopeful book about vitality in American faith communities that may not always look like faith communities. At a time when the dominant narrative about religion in America describes churches as backward and cowardly places of stagnation, this book tells the particular stories of alternative faith communities that bravely innovate to make the world a better place for all. The authors write, 'Religion cannot be franchised,' and indeed, in this brave new world, we relish the stories of creativity and independence that mark the bright future of religious expression."
—Verity A. Jones, Founder, New Media Project

TIM SHAPIRO

WITH KARA FARIS

DIVERGENT CHURCH

THE BRIGHT PROMISE OF ALTERNATIVE FAITH COMMUNITIES

Abingdon Press™

Nashville

DIVERGENT CHURCH:
THE BRIGHT PROMISE OF ALTERNATIVE FAITH COMMUNITIES

Library of Congress Cataloging-in-Publication Data has been requested.

ISBN: 978-1-5018-4259-7

17 18 19 20 21 22 23 24 25 26—10 9 8 7 6 5 4 3 2 1
MANUFACTURED IN THE UNITED STATES OF AMERICA

CONTENTS

ACKNOWLEDGMENTS

First and foremost, we want to express gratitude to the divergent churches who freely shared their time, stories, and thoughts about the work they're doing in their respective congregations. We have great respect for each of these leaders and congregations and applaud them for trying something new. They are (alphabetically by congregation name) the following: Jonathan Grace and Larry James from Church at the Square in Dallas, Texas; Tom Dickelman from The Community Church in Lake Forest, Illinois; Lisa Cole Smith from Convergence in Alexandria, Virginia; Katie Hays from Galileo Church in Fort Worth, Texas; Anna Woofenden from The Garden Church in San Pedro, California; Monique Crain Spells from Levi's Table in Indianapolis, Indiana; Timothy Kim from Root and Branch Church in Chicago, Illinois; Zach Kerzee from Simple Church in Grafton, Massachusetts; John Helmiere from Valley and Mountain in Seattle, Washington; Anne Williamson from WAYfinding in Indianapolis, Indiana; and Edwin Lacy from Wild Goose Christian Community in Indian Valley, Virginia.

We offer our thanks to our colleagues at the Center for Congregations. Their support made this book possible. Nancy Armstrong, Eunita Booker, Terrance Bridges, Matt Burke, Sofia Cook, Carol Delph, Nancy DeMott, Catharine Greene, Doug Hanner, Jerri Kinder, Katherine Lindberg, Wendy McCormick, Jane Mastin, Kelly Minas, Aaron Spiegel, Rose Villarruel, Sue Weber, Kate White, and Allison Zwickl.

Our deep appreciation goes to the Lilly Endowment, Inc. for their generous support of the Center for Congregations.

The book was helped greatly by the editing expertise of Becky Huehls of Comet Dog Studios. Thank you!

Finally, thank you to Abingdon Press for inviting us to write this book. We especially thank Constance Stella, Peggy Shearon, Paul Franklyn, and Katherine Johnston.

Introduction
WHAT IS A DIVERGENT CHURCH?

A new kind of congregation is emerging, one in which tried and true practices are expressed in creative ways. To develop innovative ways of expressing these practices, talented leaders—both clergy and laity—are developing congregations shaped by unique, contemporary expressions of time-honored religious practices.

The focus of these new, emerging congregations unfolds naturally from their setting. These congregations almost always have a focus beyond worship itself: growing and serving food, collaborating with other nonprofits, providing resources for musical and theatrical performance, befriending the homeless, celebrating Appalachian culture, and much more. The focus itself does not constitute the tried and true practices expressed in creative ways. However, the focus is upheld by time-honored practices such as shaping community, conversation, artistic expression, breaking bread, community engagement, and hospitality. The creativity comes from the stuff of the community, not from something that can be acquired off the shelf from a distant location. This juxtaposition of tried and true religious practices expressed in a highly contextualized manner leads to what we call divergent churches.

The kinds of congregations we learned from take many different forms. These divergent communities include nonprofit/congregation hybrids; multicultural communities; coffee shop, pub, and food-oriented churches; businesses combined with churches; churches focused on a particular social need like homelessness or housing; congregations of particular groups of people like cowboys or members of the Lesbian, Gay, Bisexual, Transgender, Queer (LGBTQ) community; house churches or dinner table churches; gatherings that have a spiritual intent but may or may not meet the definition of a congregation; satellites and multisites; denominational church plants that do not look like previous efforts; and so forth.

Yet, the visible innovations aren't the only creative expression of these congregations. What is most striking about these divergent congregations is how the leadership has taken a time-tested practice and made it shiny and new in their present context. Such reconstituted practices bring people closer to one another and to God.

We wrote this book as a witness for these congregations. We believe they represent a bright future for faith communities. That bright promise is born out of discontent and critique of some expressions of Christian religious life, but also—and more importantly—ingenuity, persistence, risk-taking, patience, urgency, and deep tugs on the soul for something new. The premise of this book is that people from many representations of religiosity and belief are creating faith communities that reflect the basic human need for connection to the Divine, for connection to one another, and to contribute to the flourishing of the world.

What You Will Learn

This book is about divergent churches and their practices. In introducing you to these churches, we observe their innovative forms alongside the ways these churches express human practices like shaping community, breaking bread, hospitality, artistic expression, and more. By learning from divergent churches, we have discovered that divergent faith communities are creative. These congregations worship God in vibrant ways. They also maintain intense focus on another aspect of life. We have come to call this focus on another aspect of life in addition to worship "church plus." This additional focus represents the most creative aspect of the divergent church and the place where the time-honored practices receive new life.

By reading this book, you will learn about innovation and congregational life. If you are interested in congregational innovation, if you seek creative ways to do ministry, this book is for you. If you are seeking ways to adapt tried and true practices to your setting in a way that honors the gifts of your congregation and the unique nature of your setting, this book is for you. If you seek conversation partners about exploring what a divergent congregation might look like in your setting or if you wish to adapt some of the practices in a more established setting, you will learn from the congregations depicted in this book.

We will provide you with examples of practices from divergent churches that you can consider in light of the practices of your congregation. Such comparison and contrast offers you the opportunity to reflect upon and then act on activities that represent a bright future for your congregation.

You can learn from this book by reading from beginning to end. Or you might find it more useful if you choose chapters that are of particular interest. At the end of subsequent chapters are reflection questions that are meant to be addressed with others.

Our Exploration

We interviewed leaders from thirteen congregations for this book. Although we are not researchers by vocation, we have experience working with more than one thousand congregations around almost every imaginable congregational issue. Our approach to learning about divergent congregations includes observational and qualitative inquiry. Where we name an actual clergyperson, staff person, or layperson, we have received permission to do so. In some instances, to maintain anonymity for the subjects, we have omitted or changed the names, places, and other details of an experience. In a few cases, we have created composites to preserve anonymity.

Throughout the book we write in second person. That is, we refer directly to "you," the reader. In some cases, we are imagining you participating in a divergent church's activity. Our choice to employ this act of imagination came from the highly relational and contextual nature of the divergent churches we studied. We want you to observe them as closely as you can.

We write from an admiring point of view. Although there is much to be learned from critique, we feel there is even more to be learned from highlighting strengths and assets.

As authors we are witnesses. Our writing is testimony to the good and beautiful experiences occurring in divergent congregations. Certainly, as people who are observing and writing about these churches, our perspective is inherently different from the people who are living in such faith communities. Though we may be personally participating in some ways, more importantly, we have the honor of representing a part of congregational life in the United States that's wide-awake to new things.

Meaning-Making

Through this book, we are witnesses to an awakening. We're asking others to be awake to it as well. Our aim is to demonstrate the importance of simply (or not so simply) being aware to what changes are happening and who's making them and why. Listening to another and then telling a story is a simple concept in terms of human interaction. Yet, we think bearing witness to something that is good and life-giving has an exquisite purpose.

Something essential to being human is at stake. What is at stake is more than the survival of the church. What is at stake is more than organizational vibrancy as it relates to congregational life. What is at stake is the human yearning for meaning and transcendence.

Making meaning out of life is a basic human impulse, and connecting with and understanding the Divine is part of that quest for meaning-making. Because gathering with others to experience the Divine is a basic human impulse, formalized religion and spirituality is a foundational element of human experience. Congregations aren't going away; neither is congregating. Healthy, organized expressions of religion and spirituality contribute to human flourishing.

As these divergent churches emerge with new ways to connect to the Divine, the people involved in these will touch their cities, neighborhoods, workplaces, families, and friends. Supporting the health of these expressions is both a validation of these faith communities and an immersion into vibrant religious experience.

Chapter 1
INNOVATION

A tapestry hangs on the wall of a church narthex. A member of the congregation brought the tapestry back from a trip to Europe, and the tapestry has been in the narthex since 1982. Near the center of the tapestry is a church building made of light-colored brick, similar to the church building that now holds the tapestry. The tapestry depicts green trees, rolling hills, and village life: Two men talk on a bridge, a horse draws a carriage, and chickens roam the streets. Homes surround the church.

In 1873, twenty charter members founded the church where the tapestry hangs. Between then and now, babies have been baptized, marriages blessed, and saints buried. In the 1970s, four hundred people attended worship on Sunday, but today attendance has dwindled to about fifty people. Recently at board meetings, people worry about how long the money will last. Is there enough for a full-time pastor? What if the church has to close? These questions carry a sense of loss, and the church community, like an old tapestry, seems to be unraveling. No one is to blame. It is more like nothing lasts forever—even our most cherished human connections.

On Wednesday afternoon at another church, a room called the Incubation Center is full of people. You try to count them, but people are moving too much. (Are there thirty people in this room?) The pastor points out four groups that occupy the space. The groups are all nonprofits. One nonprofit is working on reducing human trafficking. Another group represents a program for the arts in local schools. The other two businesses produce art sold for local causes. The pastor says, "We worship on Sundays, but our focus the rest of the week is all about entrepreneurship."

This congregation is a divergent church. The congregation worships God. Like most other congregations, people who participate in its life sing, break bread together, and talk about important matters. They participate in spiritual disciplines; they pray for one another and for the world. Yet, this congregation is different from the congregation with the tapestry in the narthex and other established congregations.

1

This church with its Incubation Center diverges from more established forms of congregating through innovation. This congregation that is a home for entrepreneurship represents a growing number of creative faith communities with a steadfast focus on another subject that doesn't just augment their spiritual focus but is fully integrated into a way of being the church. *The reality of what might be called "church plus another essential element of life" is the key innovation of the divergent church.* There are other creative realities of divergent churches. For example, this congregation does not own its building. It rents. There is a governing board, but there are no committees. On Sunday, people gather for worship around tables, not in pews. Some weeks, more people are involved in the Incubation Center than in worship, which the pastor sees as a positive characteristic of congregational life. "I feel like I'm a chaplain or pastor for a much larger community than our Sunday gathering." *There are many creative aspects to what we are calling divergent churches, but the primary innovation is a special focus on another aspect of life that shapes the practices of congregational life.*

The concentration of divergent churches on another aspect of life (social justice, entrepreneurship, theatre, a particular culture like cowboy or Appalachian culture) naturally leads such congregations to innovative expressions of historically rooted faith practices. In our entrepreneurial church example above, congregants participate in many practices that members of established churches do, but this community expresses practices in highly creative, contextualized ways. In this particular case, the community is made up of textures that retain the feel of the local community, not a denominational book of discipline. In fact, the characteristic texture of the interwoven threads of the community is unique. This is not a human gathering that could be represented in another setting. The essential thread has an immediacy. It could not be woven into another community without losing its essence. It cannot be duplicated.

A Steadfast Focus

A steadfast focus on a special topic, often related to the surrounding community, defines the life of divergent churches. This life is then shaped by highly contextualized practices that relate to the steadfast focus (more on practice in chapter 3). Whereas established congregations are frequently identifiable by location, religious worldview, denomination, or a leader, divergent congregations are set apart by immersion in some aspect of life that is in addition to and enhances their faith life together. This immersion might be about food, dance, gender orientation, social justice, or production of a good. The point is that advancing the spiritual search for God occurs in association with at least one other important aspect of life. The focus on some other life reality is then expressed through unique expressions of practice. Divergent congregations represent highly contextualized practices and a steadfast focus on a special topic.

The often-singular focus on a special issue or topic represents a fundamental shift in the way people participate in spiritual community. In divergent churches participants encounter what Paul Tillich calls ultimate concern, or the human quest for furthermost meaning.[1] Almost all the divergent churches we learned from attend to God, scripture, and practices of faith. Additionally, almost all the divergent churches we learned from attend to some singular, integrated emphasis that represents what matters most to the leaders and participants.

Simple Church, located in Grafton, Massachusetts, is an example of this steadfast focus. Like so many other congregations, the people of Simple Church gather for worship. They pray. They sing songs together. Scripture is studied. Yet, there's more. Much like a local restaurant in your town might state about itself, Simple Church describes itself as a farm-to-table community. The Rev. Zach Kerzee works at the nearby Potter Hill Farm. Potter Hill grows heirloom vegetables including acorn squash and black Spanish radishes. The farm produces grass-fed beef. On Thursday evenings at 6:00, some of this produce makes its way to Simple Church for a Thanksgiving-like dinner. Freshly baked bread is a central feature of that weekly dinner. That bread sustains the community as food and as a source of revenue. Zach notes, "We started baking bread just for the Eucharist at church and then people kept saying, 'Oh this is really good. We should sell it.'"

Another example of a steadfast focus is Wild Goose Christian Community in Indian Valley, Virginia. The town is in Floyd County, known for its celebration of Appalachian culture. When you visit Wild Goose Christian Community for worship, you will be immersed in the Gospel, yes, but also in Appalachian culture. What are the hallmarks of this culture? Rev. Edwin Lacy says, "The music, the crafts, the story-telling. And, when I say crafts, I mean quilting and furniture making, things that aren't necessarily just Appalachian, but in this setting have an Appalachian twist to them." Once a month the participants at Wild Goose move the chairs back against the wall, after ending the service with the hymn "We Are One in the Spirit," and they have a square dance. The Gospel is celebrated alongside rich expressions of the Appalachian ethos.

Divergent congregations juxtapose their expression of the Gospel with some aspect of their culture that matters deeply to the faith community. Such a juxtaposition represents the congregation's pursuit of an ultimate concern. The ultimate concern, whether it be the production of food or the celebration of a culture, is integrated into the faith community's search for the Divine.

In addition to a steadfast focus, divergent churches innovate in other ways. Now we will explore other aspects of innovation in divergent churches. These aspects include attention to a social good, being a home for those who have not previously experienced church as hospitable, and creative ways to explore meaning. Let's move next to social innovation.

Social Good and Innovation

In Gregory Jones's framework of social innovation, he writes, "Social innovation involves the discovery and development of strategies to build, renew, and transform institutions in order to foster human flourishing."[2] In other words, the reason for innovation is to achieve a social good, such as reducing suffering or creating opportunities for self-expression.

One congregation that represents social innovation is Convergence of Alexandria, Virginia. As an arts community that also worships (or is it a congregation that is also an arts community?), Convergence supports artists in Alexandria and beyond. If you visit, you will see a sanctuary. You will also learn how the sanctuary is used for concerts and rehearsals. In addition, Convergence hosts a black box theatre, a gallery, visual arts classroom space, and a recording studio used by a range of musicians, including opera singers, punk bands, and a cappella harmonizers. Art is supported as a natural expression of faith *and* as a social good. Convergence is an example of a church that is a social innovation.

Some divergent churches are comprehensively innovative. In these divergent churches, it is not a single program that is innovative. It is the form and function of the church itself that represents a discipline of creativity. The creativity is part of the personality of the congregation. It is temperamentally inventive.

In these divergent churches, the innovation is paired with the reality of disruption: disruptive innovation. Clayton Christensen and colleagues describe factors that make an innovation disruptive. Innovation that is disruptive attracts new participants to the product sector, not just to the company. Innovators often sustain their work with business models that are different from existing creators.[3]

This kind of disruptive innovation is evident in divergent churches as they attract people who have not previously been part of a worship community. In some cases, this means that people who identify as part of the LGBTQ population find a Christian community via a divergent church. Later in the book you will meet the Cowboy Church in Indiana. Its adherents include people who, by their own admission, would otherwise not participate in congregational life. When this happens among people who have experienced being marginalized by faith communities, the divergent church is functioning as a disruptive innovator, bringing new participants to congregations.

Harvard Business Review defines innovation as "the difficult discipline of newness."[4] It is difficult because developing something truly new is rare. The words of the Teacher, son of David, still hold true: "People may say about something: 'Look at this! It's new!' But it was already around for ages before us" (Eccles 1:10).

What makes something new is the juxtaposition of two or more things in a new way. Punk bands are not new. Recording studios are not new. The existence of

4

congregations isn't new. Yet the combination of punk bands, recording studios, and a church, as is the case at Convergence, does signify an innovation representing the discipline of newness

We've learned that innovation in congregational life has a longer history in some communities. Innovation isn't a new concept in every setting. For example, we learned that innovation among African American congregations has long been both a gift and a necessity. Dr. Felicia LaBoy taught us that because African American congregations represent a socially marginalized community, the leaders of African American congregations have had to be innovative. Clergy have had to figure out how to be bivocational. The community engagement of such congregations involves providing for social services, and additionally African American congregations have been leading innovators when it comes to social justice. It is becoming more common for congregations of all kinds (including divergent churches) to create community development corporations. The forerunners of this option are congregations in the African American community. So innovation is not a new phenomenon. In some congregational worlds, innovation—the discipline of newness for social good—has been a creative necessity.[5]

As the challenges of contemporary life are experienced in new ways by different people, innovation, or at least the language of innovation, has become more evident. We are at a juncture where disruptive innovation and social innovation create disciplines of newness in many sectors. Innovation is occurring in medicine, business, the social services, and education. Montessori charter schools are housed in public schools that previously focused on traditional pedagogy. Public health officials address the decline in the number of family physicians and the high cost of emergency room visits by training nurses and physician assistants to make house calls on the chronically ill. It turns out that the presence of a person is a powerful prescription for health. Those trying to address difficult community challenges are using new ways of problem-solving including design thinking and positive deviance.[6]

The realm of religion is not exempt from the cultural moment of innovation. Religious life is experiencing fundamental shifts in the way people participate in spiritual community and the way people understand their relationship with ultimate concerns.[7] People are experimenting with new ways of organizing the church. Bible studies in bars, online worship, gatherings with no designated clergy, sermons on the street, are just a few representations of emerging forms of congregating.

Focusing on Life

Divergent churches change the focus. Remember the tapestry of the church in the town. Imagine the tapestry animated. In this animation, at first, you see the church. From the church, you track the town's activity. People travel to and from their homes, past trees and rolling hills. Such sites signify families, relationships, vocation, commerce, and even care of the earth. Then the field of vision moves back to the church building. The bricks need tuck-pointing. The stained-glass window is damaged. The front door is closed. You want to go inside but the animation doesn't move through the closed front door. The focus is on the building. The longer the focus holds, the less things are animated. The focus has moved from vibrant life to a sealed door.

The image of the sealed door symbolizes the congregation functioning as a closed system. Church comes to refer to the inner functioning of the community and the need to sustain its current form. Church members focus on taking care of the building, arranging the committee schedule, creating the worship bulletin, paying the denominational dues, cleaning the carpets, and so forth. These housekeeping chores block the church from an essential existential function. The obstructed view deprives the church of a primary discipline related to innovation: *the discipline of making meaning out of life.* Perhaps it is inevitable, but many more established churches focus on maintaining the institution called church. The divergent churches we learned from innovate so as to focus, not on the church itself, but on life and meaning.

Divergent churches innovate in order to deepen meaning-making, which is a fundamental human impulse. Connecting with or understanding God is part of the quest for meaning-making, as is gathering with others to experience God. Therefore, communal religious experiences, or congregating, are foundational elements in human experience. However, without the discipline of newness, patterns and practices that used to be life-giving disengage from purpose. Ultimately, the tapestry unwinds. New threads creating new textures need to appear.

Divergent churches renew traditional congregational practices in order to deepen the meaning-making experience. For example, consider the practice of confession. Many congregations have a corporate confession of sin as part of the liturgy. A community confession of sin (said in unison) acknowledges that we, all of us, have fallen short of God's intentions. As a community act, reciting a confession of sin together reminds us that a group of people can impose damage on another group. Some faith communities have ancient practices of personal confession, such as a parishioner meeting privately with a priest for an examination of conscience, to ask for forgiveness, and to receive pardon.

It is less common for a *group* to consider confession together, face-to-face, and not from a pre-prepared prayer. At Simple Church, during an evening discussion about confession, Pastor Zach asks his congregation two questions. Zach says to the congregants, "Consider the function of confession, how publicly speaking your sins has an ability to hasten reconciliation and to move you into a better relationship. Are you recognizing your potential for sin? What was your view of confession as a child, and how has it grown?"

This contextualization and personalization of religious practice is common among divergent churches. The practices aren't new. Yet, practices in divergent congregations take on a homegrown feel; they are unmistakably personal and contextual.

In divergent congregations tried and true practices become brand-new. Traditional congregational activities are expressed in innovative, creative ways. The creativity comes from the imagination of talented leaders, both clergy and laity. The practices include shaping community, conversation, artistic expression, breaking bread, community engagement, and hospitality.

Remember the theologian Paul Tillich noted above. He created language to help people of faith think metaphorically. He understood the purpose of creeds and formulas and ancient rhetoric about faith. Yet, what he was determined to do in his work was create ways for people to think about ultimate concerns, existential dilemmas, in contemporary ways. He knew the power of ancient formulas to talk about Christ, grace, salvation, eternal life, confession, and forgiveness, but he also thought (and felt) that such words lose their power if they are not correlated to reality and experience. So, Tillich created phrases like "the courage to be," "the ground of being," and "ultimate concern." The courage to be: the ability to be one's best self despite or in spite of the reality of death. The ground of being: God is the source of all reality. Ultimate concern: the human quest for furthermost meaning. Divergent churches experiment with practices of faith by making them personal and true to the unique qualities of a particular community. Divergent churches are able to take on ultimate concerns because they travel light when it comes to institutional concerns. By doing so, such congregations help congregants focus on *life* and not on roles and functions of sustaining the church.

Who Innovates?

Why do some people strive for innovation? Why are some people willing to go against the grain? How is it that some people bear the discomfort of being disruptive? One reason is that such a person carries a keen sense of what's at stake if she or he doesn't innovate. It may be less clear the good that will develop from innovation. Yet, the unease with the status quo serves as a driver for creativity.

Another reason why some people, some clergy, pursue disciplines of newness relates to meaning-making. At some point, often because of some transformative experience, a clergy person stakes a claim about his or her life.

The gift of life leads you to want to make a difference. You have one life and you want it to count. This isn't a decision of hubris. It is consistent with the courage to be. The story you want to be able to tell about yourself isn't like an unraveling tapestry hanging on a dusty wall. Sometime, somewhere, possibly as part of a religious community, you had a glimpse of an ultimate concern or the ground of being. The colors of your landscape became more brilliant. It was as if you could stitch a thread from yourself to God; you experienced a connection worth sharing—a connection that transcended your own aims and linked you to human activity full of meaning. You weren't satisfied simply to keep an institution from running on empty (must we replace the furnace again?). You wanted to be at table with others talking about confession, reconciliation, being broken, and being put back together again.

Innovative congregational leaders apply their creativity because they want to provide experiences that move beyond sustaining the institution of church. Innovation isn't for the sake of doing something new. It is for the sake of deeper connection with God and with other human beings. Disciplines of newness are applied to making meaning out of life. The church, to the extent that it works loose from ties that bind attention almost exclusively to internal, operational concerns, weaves new threads in a colorful tapestry.

Conclusion

The churches we learned from had a focus on some aspect of life beyond worship. The existence of the focus and often the focus itself represents innovation. The participants in divergent churches are often people who have not been warmly welcomed in previous church experiences. In this sense, who participates in a divergent church represents an innovation. Another form of innovation is the way in which divergent churches focus on meaning-making more than sustaining an established form of being church.

Innovation takes place in many aspects of divergent church life. Worship is innovative. So is governance. Creative use of buildings is evident. However, the innovation that exists in divergent churches transcends any single activity. It is more than receiving the offering differently or changing from a financial calendar year to a fiscal year. Innovation is expressed through life-giving and meaning-making practices.

It is to the importance of practice in divergent churches that we now turn.

Divergent Reflections

1. Consider some activity in your congregation that is new. In what ways would you describe it as an innovation?

2. In what ways is your faith community like no other because of its location, because of its context?

3. Name an operational concern that is taking a lot of time and energy from your leaders. What is one thing you can do to move your attention to something related to the life of your parishioners or that is externally focused?

4. What is the ultimate concern of your church? Tell a story that represents this ultimate concern.

Chapter 2
WHAT CONSTITUTES A CHURCH?

W hat constitutes a church? Who decides what constitutes a congregation? Emerging forms of congregations diverge from the established forms. Divergent churches represent discontinuous patterns of congregating. At stake is whether or not current definitions of what signifies a church are comprehensive enough to describe the developing realities of these new forms of congregations. In this chapter we will discuss some of the traits currently used to describe what signifies a church and compare these traits to the realities of the divergent churches we studied.

There are various ways to consider what constitutes a church. For example, the Internal Revenue Service (IRS) defines a church by identifying the attributes of a church (nothing in this book should be taken as legal advice). So, one way to define a church is legally. Another way is through sociological definitions. Sociologists define what constitutes a church in order to study congregations as institutions, to explore the social goods they offer and the challenges they face.

There are ecclesial definitions too. Ecclesiology is the theological means to study the nature, structure, and meaning of the church. The Greek word *ekklesia* means a gathering of people meeting in a public place. In Christianity it means a public assembly of people attending to the story of Jesus Christ. After Saul's conversion, the author of Acts conveys this message: "Then the church throughout Judea, Galilee, and Samaria enjoyed a time of peace. God strengthened the church, and its life was marked by reverence for the Lord. Encouraged by the Holy Spirit, the church continued to grow in numbers" (Acts 9:31). The word for "church" used here is *ekklesia*, the assembly of Christians.

Let's explore more about these different ways of defining what constitutes a church, that is, the legal, sociological, and theological means.

Ways of Defining Church

The government defines what constitutes a church in order to recognize a right guaranteed by the First Amendment of the Constitution of the United States.[1] The word *church* is used in IRS documents in a generic sense. The word refers to churches, mosques, temples, and synagogues.[2] The IRS differentiates between churches and other kinds of religious organizations, including ecumenical organizations and faith-based nonprofits. According to the IRS, certain characteristics are typically ascribed to churches. Examples of these characteristics include the following:

- recognized creed and form of worship

- definite ecclesiastical government

- organization of ordained ministers

- established places of worship

- regular worship services

- gatherings for the religious instruction of the young[3]

These characteristics have historical precedence. Almost any congregation of the 1990s linked to a mainline denomination would fit the majority of the IRS-identified characteristics.

However, some of the divergent churches today do not meet the standards developed by the IRS. For example, some do not have an established place of worship or religious instruction for the young. A house church network we learned about gathers in different homes, and the leader isn't sure if what they do when they gather is Bible study or worship. No particular religious instruction for the young is provided; everyone participates together or the children play in an adjacent room. This house church network is not part of a larger ecclesial organization. Yet, the leader does consider what he leads a church. The IRS definition may not be comprehensive enough to include emerging, alternative faith communities.

Sociological Definition

What about a sociological perspective? Mark Chaves is a sociologist who studies congregations and teaches at Duke University. He notes that religious congregations have these marks: they are voluntary; they gather people, usually each week; and they do so for collective religious activity.[4] By "congregation" he means

> a social institution in which individuals who are not all religious specialists gather in physical proximity to one another, frequently and at regularly scheduled intervals, for activities and events with explicitly religious content and purpose, and in which there is continuity over time in the individuals who gather, the location of the gathering, and the nature of the activities and events at each gathering.[5]

Chaves acknowledges that there are borderline cases. A gathering could be religious but not constitute a congregation. For example, a Young Life gathering in a parent's home after school might be religious in nature, but such a gathering does not constitute a church. Those gathered are practicing their faith, but the group is not a congregation. Chaves's definition is an example of a sociological view of congregation: a definition related to the study of organizations that contribute to the common good in a unique way, the unique way being attention to the practice of religion.

Theological Definition

In addition to legal and sociological definitions of congregations, there are theological constructs. Such constructs are influenced by the experience of the one asserting the definition.

For instance, a person representing the Calvinist tradition will emphasize the church as a place where the word of God is preached and the sacraments celebrated. Someone rooted in the Wesley tradition might highlight the church as a "body of people united together in the service of God."[6]

In his book *Holy People*, liturgical theologian Gordon Lathrop offers various considerations regarding what you need in order to have church.[7] His offerings are evocative, not definitive. For example, he wonders if you need a certain kind of building. Do you need pews or burning candles? Do you need a place to store holy bread? What kind of relationship with God is held by those who gather? Do you need certain confessions of faith? Are there certain holy actions and practices required? What about authorization and credentials for clergy? Lathrop notes that exploring what constitutes church involves "a search for a community that welcomes one's own self into some association with God, a search for the truth about God in a social form."[8]

Now that we've looked at ways in which congregations have been defined, let's look at some forms of congregating that diverge from historic patterns.

Are These Congregations?

Imagine a nondenominational congregation that meets for worship in a rented warehouse. The pastor does not have a degree in religion, divinity, or theology. This particular church does not have a category of membership for its participants. A board meets twice a year to govern the activities of the congregation. There are no committees. The board has not applied for federal tax-exempt status. Churches aren't required to. However, the leaders are considering doing so because they seek to start an elementary school that focuses on the arts. Discussion about the tax-exempt status is about whether to apply as a church or as another kind of nonprofit. If this congregation applies for tax-exempt status as a school, is it still a church? And if so, in whose eyes?

Or picture a group that meets for Bible study every week. This group does not meet on Sunday. They meet on Thursday evening. The leader does have a degree in religion, a master of divinity from a denominational seminary. When the group of fifteen meets at the leader's home for Bible study, he offers an opening prayer. The group also tenders prayers of intercession after the study. However, there is no worship service. The sacraments aren't offered. No one preaches a sermon. The group doesn't sing hymns. The leader doesn't describe the gathering as a church, but some of the participants do. Is an assembly a church because someone calls it that? Or does some authority or commissioning organization need to confer that status?

Consider one more example. A new gathering that publicly calls itself a church is a program of another, larger congregation. The pastor for this new gathering is on staff at the host church. The governing board for this new community is the board of the host congregation. This new gathering worships on Sunday. The group worships at a faith-based, residential mental health facility. A sermon is preached. However, for a variety of reasons the sacraments aren't offered. Many of those who worship do so for a few weeks and then move on once they finish their hospitalization. Others return for worship almost every week. Is this gathering a ministry? Is it a program of the larger congregation? Does it function as a church?

In other realms of life, there are types of organizations that didn't exist a generation ago. At one time people in the United States had generally two choices about where to receive medical care: a doctor's office or a hospital. Now, there are urgent care clinics, specialized surgery centers, hospices, nurse-managed health centers, boutique clinics, wellness centers, and more. Some of these environments are extensions of doctor's offices; some are extensions of hospitals. Some of these environments are different enough that new language and new categories have been created to accurately describe their function and purpose. Perhaps divergent churches represent a new category of congregation that differs in function and purpose from other more established forms of congregating.

A Divergent Gathering

WAYfinding is a spiritual movement located in Indianapolis (establishing partnerships with religious organizations beyond Indianapolis). Everyone is welcome. Some people are rooted in a faith tradition, many others are not. Some believe in God, others don't. The purpose of WAYfinding is to help people love better than they did yesterday. WAYfinding sees diverse community as essential to this process. WAYfinding groups meet weekly for eight to ten weeks to discuss and practice topics that support participants in their journey to love more deeply. Topics vary from round to round. Areas of study include healthy living, seeking justice, reverence, spiritual practices, and more. For example, one round focused on the wisdom of the Twelve Steps.

Anne Williamson is the founder and director. She has a master of divinity as well as an economics degree. When describing WAYfinding, she feels it's important to note her own "Christian accent." However, she says, "We're not affiliated with any particular denomination or religion." Anne did not start WAYfinding as a church plant. As she says, "I started WAYfinding wondering if we could create a new kind of community movement that comes together around a way of being in the world rather than a particular set of beliefs."

What is WAYfinding? Is it something new? Is it a new form for which there isn't yet language that applies? Would an outside observer see it as a kind of church, but not a church that fits a current designation?

Angie Thurston and Casper ter Kuile of Harvard Divinity School consider the space between congregations and other kinds of gatherings. In their document "How We Gather," they tell of non-religious forms of community.[9] These nonreligious forms of community provide participants with a range, perhaps paradoxically, of spiritual connections. "How We Gather" represents several kinds of gatherings that attract millennials who otherwise are not drawn to established religious gatherings. Live in the Grey, Juniper Path, and Camp Grounded are among the assemblies considered. To varying degrees, these assemblies offer opportunities for personal transformation, social transformation, purpose finding, creativity, and accountability.[10] What about God? Thurston and ter Kuile write,

> The two of us are emblematic of the unaffiliated millennial population. One is personally religious but unaffiliated and the other loves aspects of religious community but doesn't experience a personal God. Language of religion and spirituality, and especially of God, would resonate, or not resonate, with each of us differently. But community would ultimately be unsatisfying for us both if it did not encompass the spiritual dimensions of existence.[11]

Is it possible to have a church that does not acknowledge the Creator? Or is it possible to have a gathering that worships God but does not consider itself a church?

Are we in an era where the very definition of religion is changing? If this is true, would it not follow that what constitutes a church is changing too?

The divergent churches we studied represent a variety of configurations. For example, in later chapters you will learn more about Church at the Square, a worshiping community that attends to the homeless and formerly homeless. This divergent church is anchored in a larger, established congregation. Sometimes it is hard to tell if it is first and foremost a worshiping community or a homeless ministry; it does both well and with great intentionality. Is it its own church or a program of the host congregation?

The Wild Goose Christian Community of Floyd County, Virginia, is connected to the Presbyterian Church (USA), but it is not a church according to Presbyterian polity. It is part of an initiative called 1001 Worshiping Communities.

The Community Church of Lake Forest & Lake Bluff does not have a creed or beliefs that participants need to adhere to in order to be members. In fact, the church does not have members.

Even as the marks of what signifies a church are changing, the majority of churches in the United States meet established criteria. Unfortunately, the social science data shows that many of these established congregations may not exist ten years from now. Will the sad, but perhaps inevitable disappearance of many congregations in the United States change how we define church? Let's explore this by looking at the dignity of established congregations alongside the emergence of new, divergent congregations we've described above.

The Worth of the Old, the Practice of Divergence

What about established forms of congregations? Are they anachronistic? Do they somehow serve a lesser function? We don't think so. After all, many established congregations have for years held an implicit purpose of helping people live more deeply into a coherent set of distinct religious claims and commitments. These religious claims and commitments weren't always sidetracked by needed attention to institutional survival. During long stretches of any given congregation's history, the commitment to loving one's neighbor, being hospitable to the stranger, being open to grace, and modeling forgiveness signified the best reality of the congregation.

Somewhere in the United States is a church established in 1904. It is constituted in a way that meets all of the IRS guidelines noted above. There is religious instruction for the young. The congregation is part of a denomination. It follows a form of worship and participants affirm a set of creeds. There is an established place for worship.

When you walk into the sanctuary, you see the names of the founders etched in the stained-glass windows. On this Sunday you count the number of people in worship. You stop at twenty-seven. The preacher has driven forty minutes from the nearest metropolitan area. She serves two days a week, Sunday and Wednesday. All but four of those in worship today are over the age of seventy-five. If you could see the latest financial report you'd see the figure is $46,235. That's how much money is in the church's savings account. The reality, the difficult reality, is that this congregation is not likely to be functioning ten years from now. What constitutes this church will no longer exist.

This doesn't mean that this church has failed. It doesn't mean that the congregants aren't faithful. If the church were to close, it wouldn't be the only one closing. Forty-three percent of congregations in the United States have less than fifty active participants.[12] The math represents a tipping point directed to demise. Despite the reality that many US congregations are at a life stage similar to a person entering hospice, the members of these congregations have studied scripture, wrestled with Christ's challenging pronouncements, offered beautiful blessings, been a sanctuary for community gatherings, and experienced transcendent moments representing the deep knowing that takes place in the borderland between heaven and earth. If *this* church building were to close, the stones would still speak of miracles and sacrifice and love beyond measure; the stones would still speak of lives lived practicing the wondrous and sometimes impossible claims and commitments of the Gospel.

At the same time, all across the country new forms of congregations are emerging. They diverge from whatever norm exists. (The norm has been disappearing for some time now, so it is difficult to articulate what the norm is.) We are not in position to define what constitutes a church. At least not yet. We first need to hear from congregations that are taking a divergent path. We need to hear what such congregations value, what they believe. Even more we need to observe what they *do*, how they practice their life together. Because to understand new forms of congregating, we need to look at a farther horizon, beyond the borderland, even beyond belief to the phenomenon of what is actually happening when people gather. This farther horizon contains the geography of practice. It is not possible just yet to define what a church is and what a church isn't. However, it is possible to bear witness to what these developing, divergent churches *do*, how people interact with God and with one another, how tried and true practices of faith are being made brand-new.

Divergent Reflections
1. What constitutes church for you? What kind of definition resonates with you (legal, sociological, ecclesial, or evocative)?

2. If you were starting a brand-new congregation, what are four activities or elements needed for you to consider the assembly to be a church?

3. In what ways do you think that innovative forms of congregating represent a reconstitution of faith?

4. Is the congregation you are part of challenged by the prospect of closing in the next five years? If so, in what ways does thinking about church differently open up possibilities or close possibilities for you?

Chapter 3
PRACTICES

A t a local Presbyterian church, Wednesday evening choir practice is coming to an end. Before people depart, the director asks the choir to pick up their hymnals and turn to hymn 76. "We haven't sung this for a while, but we will this Sunday," the director says. "Let's sing it through once." In harmony, the choir begins the first verse:

> My song is love unknown,
> My Savior's love to me,
> Love to the loveless shown
> That they might lovely be.
> O who am I
> That for my sake
> My Lord should take
> Frail flesh, and die?[1]

The singing of this hymn, on Wednesday, by the choir, represents how this congregation participates in the practice of singing. Other representations include their caroling "Masters of the Hall" every Christmas Eve; the way they sing the last verse of "Amazing Grace" *a cappella* during Lent, and their steadfast rule to not have paid soloists in the choir. Almost all congregations sing. And, like this congregation, almost all have ways of participating in music that are similar and different from other congregations.

At another congregation, on Sunday morning, the pastor is rapping, which signals the beginning of his sermon. While a backing track with drum loops and keyboard plays, he sings into a microphone, rhyming *grace, race, ace, cyberspace, marketplace,* and *embrace* (as in God's embrace). In this congregation, the practice of singing is quite different from the Presbyterian church singing "My Love Is Unknown" from the hymnal. However, despite the differences, both the choir and the preacher are participating in the practice of singing.

Divergent churches participate in many of the same practices as established congregations. However, as we will show, the character of the practices differs. It is as if the tried and true becomes brand-new. As we will discuss in this chapter, by *practice* we mean a certain kind of human activity. We mean activities that are enacted almost universally by human beings (like singing), but are expressed uniquely from setting to setting. In the stories that divergent churches' leaders tell, certain practices make prominent appearances. For many divergent congregations, essential practices include shaping community, conversation, artistic expression (which includes singing), breaking bread, community engagement, and hospitality. Each of these practices are enacted in any number of life settings; that is, they occur in situations that are commonly associated with church, and the practices have a vibrant life beyond Sunday morning and the sanctuary.

Radical Contextualization

In divergent churches practices are radically contextualized. One can't assume that the details of one divergent church's practice is familiar to another. A generation ago it was safe to assume that two particular United Methodist congregations would know several of the same hymns. In divergent churches many of the songs are written by resident composers. So, the songs have not traveled from one congregation to the next. Similarly, one divergent church rarely adapts another congregation's table rituals (the practice of breaking bread). The rituals are idiosyncratic and don't translate from one church to the next.

You could observe that this particularity is true about all human gatherings, all forms of congregating. That would be true, to an extent. Yet, the creativity, the newness, the innovation regarding any given practice in divergent churches represents an amplification of context. It is like someone has taken the landscape, the feelings, the gifts, the intention, the values of the divergent church—all those elements that shape a practice—and projected it on a large three-dimensional screen, making the particular elements of the context almost larger than life.

Say you haven't been to church since you were a child. At that time you worshiped with your parents at a Lutheran church. You were in elementary school, maybe fourth grade. You recall the flowing robe the pastor wore (what was that hanging around his neck and falling down the front of his body?). You remember looking at the stained-glass window during the sermon (so, that's what Jesus looked like). You wondered if that was real wine served during communion. These are the things you remember from being in church when you were nine years old.

You are no longer nine and now you try out a new church recommended by a friend. When you walk in to worship you are surprised to find yourself not in a sanctuary but in a small-sized banquet room with several round tables. A person is playing the mandolin and humming, not singing. The pastor walks into the room. She is not wearing a robe and there is no stole draped around her neck (you eventually learned the name of what that was called). The sermon turns out to be a conversation. In fact, the pastor speaks less than many others in the room. She asks questions. People respond at the tables. The subject of the conversation is what change you'd like to see in the community. By community, the pastor doesn't mean the congregation but the neighborhood. When it comes time for communion, *you* are asked to break the bread at your table. (Is it even legal for me to do this? Don't you have to be an ordained pastor?) After worship, dinner is served. The people who prepare the meal grew the vegetables themselves. When the gathering comes to an end, you approach the pastor and say, "I haven't been to church in twenty-two years." She smiles, gently laughs, and says, "We're not sure what we call this bunch."

In this experience there are many activities taking place. These activities are practices, essential human activities embodied innovatively, informed by a unique context. Let's name them. There are signs of the practice of artistic expression represented by the mandolin player. The practice of shaping community is embodied by the pastor (though in this church the leadership style is collaborative). The sermon represents the practice of conversation, which includes testimony and storytelling. Communion and the meal held after worship represent the practice of breaking bread together.

To understand more about the role of practices in divergent churches, let's explore more about religious practice.

Thinking about Religious Practices

Practice is how people do things. Religious practice is how religious people (or people seeking God) do things. An exploration of practice includes activities that are common to humanity. Practices common to most of humanity become religious practices when people act in such a way that their religious yearnings and commitments influence their activity.

Almost all cultures perform music. Music is part of the practice of artistic expression. One does not have to be a person of faith to sing well. The practice of singing is, thankfully, embedded in almost every culture. Yet, music performance, regardless of the culture, has a history. Artistic expression holds certain standards. For example, there are right ways and wrong ways to hold a mandolin. Music has forms and functions. There are rules to follow and rules to break. Singing as a practice can be done solo, in a room alone—a song no one will ever hear. Yet, music has its fullest life when it involves a community.

When philosopher Alasdair MacIntyre writes about practice, he means a specific kind of activity. Not all human activities are practices. Sweeping the kitchen floor is simply sweeping the kitchen floor. The same with washing dishes. However, all that is involved in taking care of one's home, what might be called housekeeping, is a practice. MacIntyre defines practice as

> any coherent and complex form of socially established cooperative human activity through which goods internal to that form of activity are realized in the course of trying to achieve these standards of excellence which are appropriate to, and particularly definitive of, that form of activity, with the result that human power to achieve excellence, and human conception of the good involved, are systematically extended.[2]

Here's a MacIntyre concept: sustaining a practice requires a community sturdy enough to hold and perpetuate the tradition of the practice. *The divergent churches we studied emphasize creating community. Within the community these divergent churches create, the practices develop existential and religious meaning.*

Consider another MacIntyre concept: standards of competency are important so that the practice doesn't distort human aspirations. It is important to recognize that practices have an intrinsic good and practices also contribute to an end or goal beyond the practice itself. *In divergent churches the goods develop from practices that are both historically rooted and contemporarily improvised.*

So, practices

- are communal

- have intrinsic value

- hold standards of excellence

- are self-perpetuating

- contribute to the common good

When people bring to bear a religious sensibility to a practice like singing, when the culture, tradition, standards, and community represent religious expression, then the practice becomes a faith practice.

For example, consider the practice of testimony (part of what we are calling conversation). One can testify to many different realities. One could testify about Jesus

Christ, but one could also testify the glories of many different things, including the latest Android operating system or a 1974 Keith Jarrett jazz album. Practices address fundamental human needs and conditions through specific acts. *Christian practices speak to fundamental human needs and conditions through tangible acts informed by the Gospel.* So the Christian practice of testimony is done by people who are bringing to bear on that activity the habits, stories, thoughts, and virtues of the Christian experience.

Dorothy Bass and Craig Dykstra serve as keen interpreters of Christian practice. The definition they offer is that "Christian practices are things Christian people do together over time in response to and in light of God's active presence for the life of the world."[3] Bass and Dykstra's definition highlights the communal nature of practice. Practices are not solo affairs. Even if only one person is speaking during the sermon, that one person's words are shaped by the listeners and a convergence of commentators, theologians, and other thought partners.

Their definition also signifies practices as human responses to God's work in the world. A practice is not a first act. It is a response to grace, love, mercy, healing, and many other spiritual goods.

For Bass and Dykstra, practices do not represent static tradition. Because God is active in the world, practices represent living habits. In our example of the Lutheran church above, the pastor delivered the sermon in an interactive manner. She used many time-tested resources of sermon preparation. The preacher followed the Revised Common Lectionary. She read a commentary written by one of her seminary professors. She referred to the writings of St. Therese of Lisieux. Yet, she adapted the form of the sermon so that it was congruent with how she perceived God working through her and the congregation she serves.

Finally, Bass and Dykstra assert that a practice leads to an end or goal that is larger than the practice itself. We observed this in many divergent churches. In divergent churches, practices support engagement in "church plus" endeavors. Practices keep them externally focused. Practices are the roadway that lead these divergent communities to a vast, uncharted world beyond the altar or pulpit.

Language, Faith, and Practice

Many of the divergent churches we learned from are distinctly Christian. Their practices—artistic expression, conversation, breaking bread, shaping community, and so forth—are directly informed by the life, death, and resurrection of Jesus Christ. Some of the churches hold an evangelical worldview. Some hold a neo-orthodox or neoliberal faith perspective. Some might self-identify as being progressively Christian.

Yet, not all the congregations hold a faith worldview easily defined by presently available terms. However, such congregations are not simply (or not so simply) spiritual but not religious.[4] Moreover, individuals in the congregation don't have such an idiosyncratic religious outlook that personal thoughts about faith function as the sole authority. Rather, the community accommodates a variety of religious outlooks. The variety is not a secret. People know that some are firm believers in God who is an active agent in life. People know that some view God from a mythic or metaphoric sense. The community is aware that some in their midst are agnostic, some atheist.

Indeed, many theological labels no longer fit divergent churches. It is hard to know what language to use. In many divergent churches the word *Gospel* denotes a guiding text, the mission of Jesus proclaimed in the Sermon on the Mount and also through his sermon in the synagogue (recalled in Luke 4:16-21).

For this book, we use practice as the orienting perspective in part because practices focus on behavior, activities, feelings, virtues, relationships, even landscapes. Belief systems inform practices, but practices are not entirely dependent on a systematic constellation of convictions. Behavior and experience often build beliefs. Practices can be constructed and deconstructed just as you might construct and deconstruct thinking, feeling, and talking about God through your lifetime.

At Root and Branch Church in Chicago, constructing and deconstructing beliefs and behaviors is the norm. The congregation spends time with the tried and true, ancient things like stories, songs, rituals, and calendars. They take their prompts from Jesus Christ, who "loved wildly and indiscriminately, and went out on dangerous, deadly limbs to show there's no other path in life than courageous, vulnerable love."[5]

Yet, at Root and Branch leaders give ancient things new forms. Gatherings include Welcome Tables the second and fourth weeks of the month. The Welcome Table experience happens in people's homes, where they share food and pass bread and wine. Face-to-face conversations take place. Is it God-talk? Yes, in a manner of speaking. Does the conversation include existential questions? Of course. Furthermore, language that deconstructs is a norm. That is, the congregation's character is such that people do not assume that there is a collective understanding of religious words.

One of the pastors is Timothy Kim. He's not from Chicago; he's from Los Angeles. He grew up in a conservative church context where words like *salvation, eternal life*, and *Messiah* were used frequently. The leaders of that church could assume that most members knew what these religious terms meant. That's not an assumption at Root and Branch. Most of the participants of this divergent church are between the ages of twenty-one and thirty-five. Tim notes, "Our discussion of theological themes is deconstructive, it's open, it allows for diversity of experience."

Yet, Tim knows that you just can't pull apart without starting a new foundation. Reconstruction begins through experience. It occurs when people experience grace, when they feel transcendence, when they come across courageous love. As Tim says,

"The shared vocabulary of our faith community is in our frank conversations, in the moments of being authentic and knowing acceptance." At Root and Branch, the practice of conversation is driven by the yearning to constitute faith that is meaningful for this time and place.

A Divergent Definition of Practice

So, now that we have started looking at the relationship between language, beliefs, and practices, we offer a definition of practice in light of divergent churches.

Religious practices are contextualized expressions of essential activities done by people who seek to thoughtfully embody their religious commitments with and for others.

Let's unpack this definition.

Religious practices are contextualized expressions . . . the plural *practices* is intentional. A practice always exists in relationship to other practices. These relationships may not always be apparent at first. However, interpreting the deeper meaning of life together includes seeing the relationship between practices. How does music inform hospitality? How does breaking bread shape conversation?

Practices are contextualized expressions in the sense that while there are standards to practices and ways to discern excellence, practices are also expressed in almost infinite ways, with many minute variables involved. The exact feel of a practice at a precise moment of time cannot be transferred exactly as it is to another place or time. Things are never exactly the same twice. The large loaf of homemade bread served at the communal dinner, made in a participant's kitchen, cannot be licensed like a trademark.

. . . *of essential activities* . . . Practices are essential because they are human activities that contribute to meaning. They contribute to individual and community well-being. Practices are proven as elemental to human flourishing. Music, healthy meals, and soul-deep conversations vastly improve participants' lives.

Practices are inherently cross-cultural, further evidence of their essential quality. One group can't claim ownership of practices. They are woven into the fabric of life. Practices have their own intrinsic value regardless of outputs and outcomes associated with them.

Practices are essential because they form meaning for a community. Religious practices form faith at least as much if not more than faith forms practice. Practices informed by one's relationship with God furnish a habitat for God. To use Tillich's language (which we introduced in chapter 1), participation in ultimate concerns (the quest for furthermost meaning) leads to experiences with the ground of being (God is the source of all reality). Participation in the practices of a religious community provides one with experiences of the Divine.

In *Seeing the Lord*, Marianne Sawicki maintains the reality that practices are not necessarily a response to God. Indeed, it is the very act of participating in a religious practice that reinforces a religious sensibility. Doing is the first act, not believing. Sawicki asserts that Gospel texts, particularly the resurrection narratives, are not so much testimonies about the risen Lord as they are guides about *how* to glimpse the risen Lord and how one participates in the life of the risen Lord. Particular protocols help one access God's eternal presence. The Source of Life is not found among the dead. The Source is found among the living, among people who are alive and doing the things that Jesus did: feeding the hungry, reciting the Psalms, talking about important matters. As Sawicki writes, "Resurrection doesn't happen to persons, it happens between and among them."[6]

. . . *done by people who seek to thoughtfully*. . . Practices require thoughtfulness. Practices require people to be conscious of what they do and why they do certain things. They are overdetermined. That is, many factors contribute to a practice being enacted in a certain way. The way a church shapes their community is informed by theology, relationships, context, feelings, temperament, scripture, other texts, experiences, social forces, and so forth. Thoughtfulness suggests that a practice can be done poorly or in such a way that it hurts relationships. Or a practice can be done well. It can be life-affirming.

. . . *embody their religious commitments with and for others* . . . The intentions of the Creator get inscribed into people's lives through practices. The Creator gets a body, if you will, when people participate in faith practices as part of a religious community. In this way, practices are relational. Practices are done with and for others. Relationships matter. The value of congregational practices can be evaluated based on the quality of the relationships between those who experience the practices together. Repeatedly we heard stories from divergent churches where the presence of the Creator was recognized in the relational space between people: in the words shared, the affirmations received, the commitments made. Practices are expressed between people. Practices are for others. In addition to the intrinsic good of singing a song well, the music adds to the flow of life, having at least an indirect and sometimes direct positive impact on others.

Yes, practices embody religious commitments and they are certainly unique and essential. In southern Indiana, the Cowboy Church illustrates the unique and essential qualities of practice. The Cowboy Church is a divergent, Christ-centered church. The pastor, Doug Hanner, is a winsome representative of the evangelical tradition.[7] The church he leads is also innovative and, like other divergent churches, focuses on an aspect of life beyond what is typically thought of as church. In this case, the concentration is cowboy culture. If you walked into that gathering space on Sunday, you would be welcomed. "Do you want something to eat? Are you going on the trail ride later?" You would hear music playing while breakfast is being served. The music is not quite Americana and not quite country. It is a kind of hybrid gospel bluegrass. Where else would you hear *this* music in exactly *this* way?

The gathering place for the Cowboy Church certainly doesn't look like church, at least not at first. But that's what it is. As you stand there with a plate of scrambled eggs and bacon, you are in the midst of religious people participating in age-old activities that hold contemporary, religious meaning. The room holds a constellation of practices, as if the stars had fallen from the sky and landed on the ground in this gathering space. Music, yes, and eating or breaking bread together is taking place. Storytelling or testimony is happening as well as conversation about both mundane and deep matters. *Do you have that new saddle broken in yet?* And, *It has been a month since Jillian died and my heart is still heavy.* This is human community seeking the ground of being. And it is taking place through the expression of several practices among a one-of-a-kind community.

Spiritual Habitat

Practices are highly contextual—think homegrown. They are often improvised. Practices are often the expression of the intuitive sense of the right thing. Given these characteristics of practices in divergent churches, there is another thought partner to consider in addition to MacIntyre, Dykstra, and Bass. That person is Pierre Bourdieu.

In *The Logic of Practice,* Pierre Bourdieu describes everyday life activities in the context of *habitus,* a Latin term that Bourdieu defines as the "system of structured structuring dispositions."[8] This quote is signal enough that Bourdieu is rough going. Philosophers don't always lay a smooth road. It is a long journey from a French philosopher to Cowboy Church. Yet, his observations help us understand what is occurring in alternative faith communities. Structured, structuring dispositions is a way to say that practices involve both an established set of rules and an improvised feel for the activity at hand.

Though it is not a perfect analogy, one could view the *habitus* as the field, the ground, the landscape: all that contributes to the context in which one participates.

For the Cowboy Church the *habitus* could be pictured as concentric circles. The outside circles include Christian history and Western culture. The next circle, heading inward, includes elements of the Nazarene tradition, activities related to horse riding, the etiquette of trail riding in general. The innermost circle is where, in a divergent church, the action is. Everything in the inner circle is unique, local, tied to the local community. It involves the names and faces in the breakfast dining room. It includes the meeting place. It includes the dialect spoken and the internal world of participants. This is the *habitus* of the Cowboy Church and the most influential part of the *habitus* includes the people, place, gifts, attitudes, and feelings of the people in the room (or on the trail) at any particular moment.

Expressed within the *habitus* is practice. In fact, the *habitus* produces practices. A *habitus* could theoretically produce an infinite amount of possible, even inevitable activities. Practices are both inevitable and potentially possible. This paradoxical statement is important to Bourdieu's description of life activity. Bourdieu states that the *habitus* has "an infinite capacity for generating products, thoughts, perceptions, expressions and actions."[9] Certain contexts will produce particular activities.

However, in any *habitus*, a practice also contains improvisational and extemporaneous elements. These elements are deeply rooted in the stuff of the community, reflect a discipline of newness, are sometimes spontaneous, and are occasionally involuntary. The improvisational character of practice has more in common with "feel" than it does with intention.

Ellis Marsalis, the exceedingly gifted jazz pianist, was asked by a student after a concert how much of what he and his band just played was written down. "No more than 25 percent," said Mr. Marsalis.

Ask a divergent church pastor how much she is doing is part of a planning process. She might well answer, "Hmm, no more than 25 percent."

What are the implications of this for innovative faith communities? Bourdieu's model of practice considers several threads of influence that produce any particular practice. The notion that practices proceed from a *habitus* suggests that influences for any particular practice are contextually determined and multifaceted. A subtle change in the tone of the preacher may shift the way something is received. Manners, childhood memories, the way your body feels on a particular day, the last book you read, who you are with right now, who you were with five years ago, the way the wind blows, all influence practice. The way the scrambled eggs are served at the Cowboy Church (with a smile, warm, not too much wait) may be the thing that creates the opportunity space for an authentic inventory of loss regarding Jillian's death. It is not unusual for a divergent church to pay attention to behaviors at this granular of a level.

The smallest thread can change the entire tapestry.

If this chapter had its own Spotify playlist, you'd hear a century-old hymn tune titled "Love Unknown." Click forward and you'd hear a rap with lyrics about God's grace. To the next tune, and listen to a guitar and banjo-driven bluegrass gospel song. There's the mandolin too, though what he was humming wasn't written down. The music itself is a marker of divergence. This is far beyond the debate between traditional or contemporary worship. This is about homegrown music. The music represents innovation, creativity; it has a native feel to it.

Innovation and practice form congregational experiences in all kinds of churches. In divergent churches, innovation and contextualization give practices a heightened reality. Innovation and the ramped-up importance of context create forms of congregating that may not look like other kinds of churches.

In the following chapters we introduce you to divergent churches and the practices most prominent in their faith communities. The specific practices include shaping community, conversation, artistic expression, breaking bread, community engagement, and hospitality. We could have chosen other ways to describe these new, alternative congregations. We chose to tell the story of these divergent churches through the frame of practices because we wanted you to experience what they *do*, how they function, how they form their life together. They improvise. Yet their improvisations are rooted in traditions. They enact practices in response to God's grace. Yet sometimes it is the practice that reveals the beauty of God. More than anything else, the practices of divergent churches connect participants to the Divine and to one another. Come along. You are invited. These divergent churches have a place for you.

Divergent Reflections

1. What are three key practices in your congregation? Here is a list of possibilities: shaping community, conversation, artistic expression, breaking bread, community engagement, hospitality, learning, discernment, Sabbath keeping, and honoring the body. Tell a story to someone about one of these key practices.

2. How does location shape a key practice in your congregation? What would this practice look like if it was enacted in another location? For example, how would Bible study be different if it occurred in a park rather than a room in your church building?

3. What aspects of your congregation's life together are improvised? How are these activities stronger because of improvisation? Are there ways that improvisation lessens the activity's impact?

4. If you were given full license to innovate regarding a practice, which practice would you choose and what would the innovation look like?

Chapter 4
THE PRACTICE OF
SHAPING COMMUNITY

A ll organizations have some kind of form, including congregations. Elements of form include location, roles and functions, and how finances are handled. A congregation's form is also made up of less tangible elements like the values it espouses. These elements *shape* how congregations operate as a community. This chapter is about the practice of shaping community in divergent churches.

Shaping community is a fundamental practice around which the other divergent practices revolve (conversation, artistic expression, breaking bread, community engagement, and hospitality).

Is the practice of shaping community different in divergent churches from more established congregations? That was a question we brought to our study. We observed that divergent churches possess pronounced clarity about their mission, vision, and values. Divergent churches have nimble structures, roles, and functions. Where the gathering takes place is closely connected to the congregation's identity. Compared to established congregations, many divergent churches address conflict more openly. Adherents and clergy leaders are more willing to carry the discomfort of disagreement and difficult feelings.

All congregations have a shape. Almost all congregations are fashioned by the following considerations:

- The *mission* or mission statement describes the congregation's reason for being.

- The *vision* of the church is how the world and church would be different if the church lived up to its highest ideals.

- The *values* of the congregation represent what the congregation believes and how it behaves when it is functioning at its best. In many divergent churches, innovation is an important value.

- The *structure* is represented by the decision-making relationships between congregants, staff, board, committees, and teams.

- *Roles* and *functions* create the contours of the shape of a congregation. What is the pastor's role? How are the gifts of laity honored?

- *Location* shapes community. Place includes where the congregation assembles. It may be broadly defined as city, town, suburb, or country. It may be more specifically defined as the sanctuary, someone's home, a street corner, another public place—wherever congregants are assembling.

- How the congregation handles *finances* creates a culture, typically on a continuum of scarcity to abundance. This culture contributes to the way of life congregants experience.

- Every congregation has norms about handling *conflict*. These norms form the degree to which vulnerability, transparency, challenge, anger, and other feelings are considered acceptable and helpful.

Consideration of these dynamics is part of the religious practice of *shaping community*. Life together requires structure. Every community, whether it be family, town, school, or church, needs structure so that it can function in a coherent and dependable way. Chaos does not contribute to flourishing. We make better use of our gifts when there is a consistent arrangement to communal life.

From divergent church leaders we heard several stories that highlighted aspects of the shape of a community. Most frequently the stories represent the importance of a clearly defined mission and vision along with careful consideration of roles and functions. We also heard repeatedly about the role innovation serves in the congregation's development. The third theme we heard repeatedly involved the high value for transparency and vulnerability when addressing challenges and conflict.

Let's explore how these elements of shaping religious community are expressed in divergent churches. We will begin by learning more about a congregation that is committed to clarity about roles and function as well as mission, vision, and values.

Shaping Communities around Spiritual Refugees

Galileo Church in Texas is a divergent church. It fits many of the defining characteristics of a faith community. The community of Galileo attends to God. Disciples at Galileo seek to follow Jesus. The congregation is a member of the Christian Church (Disciples of Christ) denomination. Yet, it attends to another great thing in its midst, a mark of a divergent church. This other great thing they strive for is to form a community that can be a home for *spiritual refugees*. Being a home for spiritual refugees includes doing justice for and with LGBTQ people. It includes kindness to people with mental illnesses or in emotional distress.

These great things are supported by another value: "We do real relationships; no bullshit ever," states lead evangelist Katie Hays and other leaders at Galileo.[1]

It's not easy to maintain relationships absent of bunk and drivel. It's not easy to live out the beautiful things espoused on Sunday through real life on Monday. Yet, wherever and whenever the Galileo community gathers, you will see people trying as hard as they can to tell and live the truth. This faith community wants to live its values. This divergent church isn't designed around the idea that merely stating its values is enough. The people of Galileo intend to make real its mission, vision, and values. In the language of the community, Galileo "does beauty for our God-Who-Is-Beautiful." Katie says, "We try every single week in worship to create beautiful art and make beautiful sounds and set a beautiful table. God appreciates beauty—just look around! And made in God's image as we are, we really can't help but make more of what God enjoys."[2]

When Galileo's co-conspirators (this church's name for covenanted members) seek to do life together, there are echoes of Dietrich Bonhoeffer and his focus on the hard work regarding life together as Christian community. As Bonhoeffer wrote from prison, "I mean living unreservedly in life's duties, problems, successes and failures, experiences and perplexities. In so doing we throw ourselves completely into the arms of God."[3]

Galileo Church's mission is to be a home for spiritual refugees; it is to be an honest community lifting up the beauty of God and the beauty of the faith community. Following these virtues has led the Galileo community to adapt roles and functions, more naturally and more creatively than such adaptation takes place in most established congregations.

Nurturing the Spiritual Community

Rev. Dr. Katie Hays's role has changed at Galileo over a relatively short period of time. Katie's first role was church planter. Then she was the nascent church's pastor. But as Katie says, "The leadership team essentially fired me as pastor and rehired me as lead evangelist." Of course the "firing" didn't mean that Katie left Galileo. It was the community's way of recognizing the evolution of Katie's role and function. The designation of lead evangelist signaled that the church wanted to keep its focus on seeking out spiritual refugees. After twenty years of serving as pastor in traditional church settings, Katie observes that it was all too easy for her to settle into the role of taking care of the people who were already present at Galileo. However, Galileo Church seeks to be a community of faith that can follow God when God takes, as Katie calls it, a hard left turn. So Galileo Church "fired" Katie as pastor and made her lead evangelist to signify the church's ongoing commitment to, as they say, "the people who are not here yet."

The change in Katie's role led to a change in organizational structure. Katie and her co-conspirators initiated two new teams: the Missional Logistics Team and the Care and Feeding Team. The Missional Logistics Team is charged with helping the whole community keep its focus on Galileo's unique attention to spiritual refugees, as well as its attention to being an honest community lifting up the beauty of God and the beauty of the faith community. The Care and Feeding Team provides pastoral care to those who are already part of Galileo and helps guide the congregation's deepening discipleship of Jesus.

So, the shape of Galileo's faith community includes a lead evangelist, a Missional Logistics Team, a Care and Feeding Team, and missional priorities that support ministry with spiritual refugees and a culture of honesty. Let's now look at the activities of Galileo.

Putting the Mission into Practice

Sunday is an important day for Galileo. Yet, as is often the case in the divergent churches we studied, weekly worship does not occur on Sunday morning. Community life begins at 3:00 on Sunday afternoon with G-coffee. This gathering, led by a ministry intern, meets at a McDonald's. The intern has a Galileo credit card and buys coffee or ice cream for whomever shows up, as it is a feature of Galileo gatherings that one should never have to wonder if a G-gathering will be affordable. You will see others with knitting needles and yarn or coloring books and bright pencils. Welcome to a time for conversation and fellowship.

At 3:00 p.m. there are additional gatherings at the rented Big Red Barn in Kennedale, just south of the Forth Worth city limits. Like other divergent churches, Galileo doesn't own a building, nor does it want to.

G-Kids and G-Youth are led by the evangelist for youth and several volunteers; all school-age kids are invited to come share life, pray together, and explore the scripture that will be read in worship later. G-Sunday is a biblical-theological class for adults, usually led by Katie, where a "rehabilitative theology" is offered for spiritual refugees who carry damaging teachings from their early experiences in Christian community. At 4:00 p.m. the musicians, the worship tech person, and the set-up team arrive. There is a bustle in the Big Red Barn as sound checks begin, computers are connected, candles are lit, and the communion table is set.

Worship begins at 5:00 p.m. and it is meant to be beautiful (for our God-Who-Is-Beautiful). The lighting is ambient and dim. The music is homegrown. Worship often features music written specifically for worship at Galileo. There are pillows for kneeling for prayer. At the prayer wall, made of wooden pallets, you can tuck your written prayers into the slats.

This worship experience could only come from the specific context and constellation of relationships that comprise Galileo. It is an example of the intensely contextual experience of many divergent churches (and the power of what Bourdieu calls, as described in chapter 4, the *habitus*). That is, the prayers and songs are not typically out of a denominational prayer book. They come from the souls and the stuff of the community itself. Yes, there are songs, many of which are traditional Protestant hymns but reworked for these singers. And there is a sermon. But there is also a guided reflection time in response to the biblical and theological theme of the evening. Those gathered are encouraged to *do* something: write, draw, or create something in response to the sermon.

The Lord's Supper is offered every week. After all, as Katie Hays reminds us, "Jesus ate all the time and with everybody." So, at Galileo "all, absolutely all, are welcome at that Table." This unconditional invitation is consistent with John Dominic Crossan's view of open commensality: the pattern of breaking bread together that disturbs societal discriminations and separations that are often visible when we eat with one another.[4]

The way in which food is shared and worship is designed, the way in which Galileo owns no buildings and steadfastly looks out for and does life with the spiritual refugee (especially this) constitutes a Christian practice. This practice is shaping community.

The practice of shaping community at Galileo is elegant in its intentionality. This divergent church isn't simplistic. It isn't facile. If the community construct represents clarity, it is because Katie Hays and the other lay leaders have worked hard to make life together lucid in the midst of complex challenges. We can picture the development of community at Galileo moving from void (at creation) to chaos (at times) to complexity, then to transparency, and now there is a kind of hard-earned graceful life-world. The essence has become apparent. The essence is beauty (because God is beautiful), honest relationships, and the safety of home for the spiritual refugee.

Shaping Community through Innovation

A unique challenge for the divergent church is how to remain creative and nimble while also addressing constraints. It is one thing to remain in the bliss of early

Eden. It is another to shape a community sturdy enough to support people to address the ever-increasing challenges of life over time. An emerging challenge for creative, alternative forms of congregations is how to negotiate seasons beyond commencement, so that the community moves beyond idealized expectations to changed lives. To explore these developmental challenges, let us introduce you to the Community Church of Lake Forest & Lake Bluff.

The Community Church of Lake Forest & Lake Bluff, located in a suburb near Chicago, Illinois, is the oldest of the divergent churches we studied. Rev. Tom Dickelman led the first worship service in September 1999. Back then the church was known as the Community Worship Hour. Worshipers gathered at the chapel on the campus of Lake Forest College. The chapel, called the Lily Reid Holt Memorial Chapel, is not the kind of gathering space you might associate with an alternative faith community. The chapel was built in 1900 (now a National Historic Register Landmark). It is made from Indiana limestone and inside contains a Tiffany stained-glass window and five Tiffany hanging lamp fixtures.[5] When you walk in you might think it is the home for a long-established Presbyterian church, not a worshiping community that turns many assumptions of church inside out.

A Focus on Worship

How did Tom come to develop the Community Worship Hour in 1999? In 1992, Tom was in a doctor of ministry program. One day, Tom posed a question to his advisor. "What would it look like if a church didn't focus on growth but on doing a few things really well?" Tom was thinking, What would it be like if there was a micro-church like a microbrewery? Microbreweries aren't interested in making the most beer. Brew masters at micro-breweries want to make high-quality beer. In similar fashion, what might a "micro-church" look like?

Tom waited eagerly for his advisor's response. After reviewing Tom's idea, his advisor said, "For starters you can't do this for your thesis. And second it will never work."

"I was so angry," remembers Tom.

Tom shelved his idea and continued ministry in traditional church settings, which included two of the largest Presbyterian Church (USA) congregations: Fourth Presbyterian Church of Chicago and Second Presbyterian Church of Indianapolis.

However, the idea of the micro-church never left his soul. Through his work as a pastor, Tom knew he didn't want to be on his deathbed someday regretting all the stuff he never tried. Tom felt the need for a micro-church not only inside himself, but also when he looked outward and considered the North Shore area of Chicago. So, seven years after submitting a proposal to the advisor, Tom began the Community Worship Hour.

The new community took shape. There wasn't a building. They rented the Lily Reid Holt Memorial chapel. There were no committees. Eugene Peterson once said rather wryly, "I had a friend—he's dead now—and committee meetings were his forte."[6] There were no members. There wasn't a long list of programs trying to meet the needs of every age group and life experience. The community was to be about worship.

This was a new church start. But it wasn't like other denominational new church starts at the turn of the last century. After all, there was no denomination funding the work. Tom and his household self-funded this project (through a second mortgage). This was not a Presbyterian Church (USA) church plant, though that was the denomination that held Tom's credentials. The goal wasn't to establish an independent megachurch. This new gathering was, however—for sure—a worshiping community.

In the hundred-year-old chapel this new community worshiped on Saturdays at 5:00 p.m. Like other divergent churches, this gathering included people who, for various reasons, did not feel at home in other churches. The assembly welcomed people from the north suburbs of Chicago who wanted to seek God but without the trappings of more established churches (committees, building upkeep, aggressive fundraising, and so forth).

People came. But not a lot of people. If Tom was concerned about resisting the megachurch temptation, he didn't need to worry much.

"I would look out into the chapel and see about eleven people on one side and another eleven on another. Enough for a football scrimmage," recalls Tom.

At this point in its creation, the Community Worship Hour was experiencing a tension that many divergent churches experience early in their histories. The tension is that to begin an innovative, new ministry it often takes the charismatic vision of one person. However, to sustain such a vision, the divergent church inevitably needs to maintain the innovative vision *and* bring other leaders into the fold to collaborate, all the while maintaining the nimbleness of the early days. This pivot is an almost impossible task. It is also a necessary task if a divergent church is going to last beyond five years.

A Dedication to Innovation

One resource Tom had was innovation itself. You may recall that in chapter 1 we shared a definition of innovation from the *Harvard Business Review:* "Innovation is the difficult discipline of newness." When leaders think about and act upon innovation the emphasis is often on *newness* and not on *discipline.*

Through years of theological training and work as a business consultant, Tom thought (and prayed) about innovation. For Tom, innovation is an actionable idea that "brings back." What he means by "bring back," is that there are results. Something is achieved. There is impact. People's attitudes and behaviors change. The fact that something is new is not enough. The discipline to bring about results is an essential component of innovation.

After about three years it was clear that the Community Worship Hour was new and creative, but there weren't results. Even if you don't intend a megachurch, you need to have at least some people showing up.

It isn't easy to admit that your dream isn't working. At the end of the third season of Saturday evening worship services, Tom sat on the back steps of the chapel.

"I cried like a baby," remembers Tom.

He was at the end of this particular desert journey. He was thirsty. He was stranded on dry land. His innovative dream needed to take a different shape in terms of action and results. This moment on the steps was a kind of epiphany event for Tom. It was the beginning of clarity about changes he would make over the next several months.

First, he knew what would not change. They were not going to purchase a building. No one would ever become a member. This alternative community was going to continue to be denominationally nonaligned. There were going to be no new committees (at least until absolutely necessary). The focus was still going to be on worship.

Tom began listening to feedback. For a while people had been telling him that the name for the gathering—the Community Worship Hour—didn't communicate the unique marks of the experience. "You are a church," he was told. "Go ahead and claim it."

So, what changed? The name changed. The Community Worship Hour became the Community Church of Lake Forest & Lake Bluff.

What else changed? The gathering time changed. No longer would they gather on the seventh day. They moved the worship time to Sunday morning, the Lord's Day.

In terms of leadership dynamics, elements of the solo journey were coming to an end. Tom maintained his charismatic vision, yet he paused more often to consider feedback. This community structure would remain nimble. Tom was still empowered to make decisions free from endless committee transactions. But Tom was more open to the opinions of others.

As the Community Church further developed, Tom and other leaders began to think more strategically about finances. The no-committee rule loosened just a little. A group of leaders were assigned the responsibility of overseeing the finances. These leaders and Tom chose not to see money as taboo or evil. (The scripture quote is *not* that money is the root of all evil; it is the *love* of money that is problematic, per 1 Timothy 6:10.)

Tom says, "I believe one has to be as passionate about the economics of innovation as the creative, spiritually fulfilling side of innovation."

Because of this thinking, the Community Church is still free from dependence on denominational funding.

During the early years, as the Community Worship Hour, the community gathered from fall to spring. During summer, everyone—Tom, the music leader, the worshipers—took a sabbatical. There was no worship during the summer months; to sustain the fall-to-spring schedule required so much energy (and money) that Tom and others needed to take a deep breath during June, July, and August. This break was good for emotional well-being. However, the momentum of gathering together was snapped each year. Every September it was like starting completely new all over again. The decision to worship all year was made (another sign Tom was listening to feedback).

Then one more thing changed. It made all the difference. The change had to do with where the church would assemble.

The decision had been made to worship all year long but the chapel wasn't available during the summer. So, where?

Tom wandered. He explored different sites. One day he was walking the beach in Lake Bluff on Lake Michigan. He came across his favorite place on the beach. That day at his favorite place he had a revelation.

This was to be the place.

Not only was this spot of beach a special place for Tom, it was a place known and loved by many people in the community. Why not worship in one of the most special places in this community? Tom knew that on any given summer Sunday he could arrive early and claim the location for his people. Before the lifeguards arrived, before others staked their territory, Tom would create a worship space, a tabernacle of sorts, there on the beach, Sunday at 8:00 a.m.

If you are there early enough you can see them coming. There's a grandfather, his daughter, and grandchildren paddling toward the shore in a kayak. Someone is putting up a multicolored rainbow umbrella (this is a super-sized umbrella) to shield the kids from the sun. Members of a ukulele band are walking down to the beach, their instruments in hand. On this Sunday you will see the waves roll in and out (the wind is just the right amount). Tibetan prayer flags fly from the open-air shelter, winding and rolling with the wind. Most summers, worshipers go to the water's edge for a walk-on-water contest for children.

The Community Church of Lake Forest & Lake Bluff started as a micro-church, Tom Dickelman's response against the institutionalized and established larger congregations.

"Don't get me wrong," says Tom. "These congregations are so very important. They just aren't for me and for many of our community."

Now, on Easter—early enough in the year that they are still at the chapel—Tom will look out at almost five hundred people in attendance during *two* services.

It will never work, a micro-church like a microbrewery.

But then again, it just might.

Vision, Values, and Congruence

We are exploring the practice of shaping community in divergent churches. We have learned how the Community Church of Lake Forest & Lake Bluff is both innovative and nimble. Through the years, many things have changed, including its name and meeting place. Earlier in the chapter we learned about Galileo Church's dedication to spiritual refugees and how it has adapted its organizational structure to fulfill its mission.

Now let's explore how Galileo, as a divergent church, addressed a challenge, a conflict, in a way consistent with its vision and values.

Church leaders say beautiful things. *You are loved. You are forgiven. Blessed are the peacemakers. Blessed are the poor. Christ is risen.* The words are like smooth chalices in a pottery shop with the sun shining in through the window.

One attribute of divergent churches is that these beautiful messages are embodied in the community. Of course, many congregations hold this desire—new, old, established or alternative, evangelical, mainline, or progressive. Many churches strive to shape their assembly so that behaviors match their beautiful messages. This desire is intensified in divergent settings. Maybe the intensity comes from the character of the leaders. Or perhaps the intensity is present because those who created the ideals (so recently) are active as opposed to a more established congregation in which the founding vision is like a distant horizon in the rearview mirror.

In divergent churches, practicing what is preached is an everyday exercise. The contours of the divergent community are designed by integrity, authenticity, and the congruency between words and actions. To stand by one's word—that is a goal of the divergent churches we studied.

Is the intensity around congruency of word and action naiveté, idealism, or a hard-earned forthrightness? Perhaps it is a combination of multiple dynamics. Many divergent church leaders have experienced the complacency of more established churches. Clergy of alternative faith communities are seeking a religious community for themselves and others where authenticity is upheld. For example, the prayer of confession isn't an empty ritual. Remember when not too long ago new church planters were coached *not* to include a prayer of confession in the liturgy? People don't want to feel bad about themselves, clergy were advised. In divergent churches, the prayer of confession signifies the desire for comprehensive and sometimes painful honesty before God and one another. Such honesty is a sign of a community shaped by the desire for congruence between beautiful messages and actual behavior.

Congruence Is Tested

Let's revisit Galileo Church. It values relationships, honest communication, with a priority of "no bullshit, ever." It sees itself as a safe harbor for spiritual refugees because of God's expansive welcome. What happens when a divergent church's highest values are tested? How does the shape of the community change?

Katie Hays, the lead evangelist at Galileo, describes a situation where the church's effort to live consistent with its values didn't go well. As Katie says, "It didn't work out in a really big way."

The phone rings. Katie answers. A man says, "I really would like to come to your church. Can I meet with you?"

Katie says, "You don't have to meet with me. Just come on over. Everybody is welcome."

The man says, "You don't understand. I have to meet with you before I can come to church. I'm a registered sex offender."

A registered sex offender can pose logistical and legal challenges for any congregation. For example, the man's sex offender status might outline certain restrictions. In addition to complying with the law, the congregation may have a unique challenge around the issue of disclosure, especially in a church that values transparency.

Katie learns more. The man lives in town. He seeks friendship having the last several years alienated from others because of his sexual offense. And the man is gay. As authors we note his sexual orientation as a fact and because it adds to Galileo's challenge of wanting to honor its mission of being a spiritual home for the LGBTQ community. We want to be clear *not* to evoke the false stereotype that gay men are somehow more likely to be sex offenders.

Katie knows this situation is going to be complicated. Yet, her immediate thought is this feels like Galileo's work to do. At the communion table each week the words are spoken: "All are welcome at the table of our Lord." Galileo's stated mission is to seek spiritual refugees, especially LGBTQ people. The church's stated mission is to do kindness for people in emotional distress. So, Katie is thinking, how do we do this work that is clearly ours to do?

Given the shape of the community, both within Galileo and beyond, there are things Katie can do. She acquires the permissions needed to talk with his probation officer and court-appointed psychologist. She goes to the Missional Logistics Team, the group that helps the church remain committed to its missional priorities. The response from the Missional Logistics team is fully human. *This is hard work. We kind of wish it would just go away. Yet, this is our calling so let's figure out how to do it.*

41

Katie shares the same information with the Care and Feeding Team, which if you recall, was set up to allow Katie to focus on being an evangelist. The man's request raises pastoral care questions in addition to the missional and logistical questions. Prayers are said. Tears are shed. This is difficult. The meeting is difficult because there are people present who have been hurt by sexual assault and chronic abuse, and everyone knows someone who has suffered this pain. Not just a few people have been hurt. It seems that at Galileo there are many people who have been hurt by others. (Is this true because Galileo draws such people, or are people at Galileo more willing to talk about this important issue?) The leaders on both teams ask for time to think and pray about the issue of welcoming this person.

As happens in human community, no matter the shape and construct, the more people involved in the process, the more opportunity for misunderstanding. This occurs at Galileo. The message received beyond the core group of leaders is that "Katie has invited a pedophile to our church," which is not the case. Yet, the spread of this message intensifies the difficulty of the original challenge.

What began as a difficult challenge that seemed possible given the congregation's values becomes a conflict revealing gaps between the beautiful vision of the congregation and reality. Katie can feel the movement. The community has shifted from "we can do this, we need to do this" to "there is way more work that needs to be done for us to be able to welcome this person."

"This is much bigger than I knew," says Katie.

What would you do? What do you do when your church faces a challenge that is at the core of your identity and you wish you didn't have to face this moment of truth?

The Mission Is Reevaluated

Discernment is the work that Katie moves to next. This means more conversations with the Missional Logistics Team and the Care and Feeding Team, and many conversations with Galileo people outside those teams who are survivors of sexual assault and abuse. It means that after much prayer, sleepless nights, and necessary conversations, Katie recommends to the other leaders that, painfully, Galileo will need to say no to the man because the community is not ready—and perhaps, due to the nature of the church's mission to make safe space for one kind of spiritual refugee, Galileo will never be a place that such a person can find a home.

As Katie reflects, "We need to back way up and do some relational and discipleship work before we get to this, because we could hurt this guy for real by welcoming him when we're not ready. And we could hurt some people in our church for real by doing this before we've thought more about what this means for them."

It meant that Katie found another congregation for the man, a traditional church that has already welcomed registered sex offenders and has a program ready-made. Katie reflects, "Why did I think we were the only ones who could befriend him?"

Katie spent more time with her co-conspirators. She listened to their stories. She was back, at least for the time being, to serving functionally as their pastor and not exclusively the lead evangelist.

The whole story is told to the entire faith community in a Sunday night worship service, through a litany written by Katie and spoken by all the leaders on the Missional Logistics Team and the Care and Feeding Team. Though Galileo has always honored open conversation, this conversation was unlike any they had experienced. Difficult questions are raised that are not easily answered. For example, some in the community were questioning whether they should be standing behind the communion table and saying "*all* are welcome." What does "all are welcome" mean now that someo*ne wasn't* welcome?

The litany included a prayer of confession. Within a few steps of the communion table, different people took turns speaking to the assembly:

This is one of those decisions
where nobody is happy.
Some in our church will be disappointed
that we were not more courageous
and more faithful to the gospel
of reconciliation and love.

Some in our church will be hurt and angry
that we even considered saying yes,
even though we decided to say no.
You'll think we are unwise,
or inconsiderate of your suffering.

So we are also confessing
our fear that our church is not
strong enough to bear the weight
of this awful moment.

But we would not keep it from you.
We are asking you to help us
bear what has happened.
Your leaders need your help.[7]

43

There is a desire in life within and beyond the church to preserve that which is shiny and new, to want to remain in Eden. The divergent churches we studied have created virtually pristine ways of handling the messiness of life with God. Life in a divergent church can feel unspoiled and pure. It can feel as though one has discovered an enhanced community of faith, a faultless alternative to the megachurch and the established church and the dying church.

However, what is truly special about the shape of community in the divergent church is not the illusion of purity. What is special is the tenacity of honesty. These divergent churches are not self-absorbed. They are self-aware. This self-awareness comes at a price. Dietrich Bonhoeffer wrote, "It is much easier to see a thing through from the point of view of abstract principle than from that of concrete responsibility."[8]

Katie Hays and the other leaders were disappointed in the shape of their community. They felt they had not been true to the very values they espoused. Yet, there was one value to which they were resolutely true: honesty. It may be true that at any given time during this difficult journey, the co-conspirators of Galileo were reticent with their truth-telling or found that shared words were too fragile for the community to hold safely. However, over the entire arc of the challenge, the situation was examined closely in juxtaposition with the deepest values of the community. If at some points the words, the feelings, the actions fell out of alignment from the values of the community, the presence of transparency powered the community to make adjustments and come to what they called the "least worst" decision they could make. Sometimes in faith and life, you choose your disappointment. Doing so is an act of honesty. And you are living in a landscape of truth and beauty.

Divergent Distinctives

Earlier in the chapter we asked the question: Is the shape of community different in divergent churches from more established congregations? To be clear, the difference between divergent churches and established churches is not an all or nothing proposition. However, as we examined narratives about divergent churches and the shapes of their communities and the experiences we've had working with established churches, we offer some distinctions.

Divergent churches are guided by original principles expressed through mission, vision, and value statements. Such claims and commitments are taken seriously. They are referred to frequently. They serve as rules of life not unlike the rules of life for a monastery or convent. In more established churches, statements about mission, vision, and values sometimes sound borrowed from a template. In divergent churches people dive deep into their values, risking lost sleep over gaps between stated values and actual behavior.

Divergent churches are spry when it comes to adjusting their organizational structure to meet the demands they face. Their organizational charts are simple. They are written in pencil, not pen. Furthermore, in divergent churches, changing organizational structure and adjusting roles and functions have measurable results and impact. In more established congregations, tinkering with structures and functions often results in a surface change, a change on paper represented in a policy manual, but frequently fails to yield changes in attitudes, in behaviors, and over all flourishing.

The practice of shaping community creates churches in which values are held deeply, changes are made promptly, and disagreements are addressed directly. A practice that informs these activities (and more) is the practice of conversation: how people talk with one another about that which is most important. In our next chapter we move from observing the shape of the community to the importance of conversation. Let's prepare to listen to divergent churches as their adherents talk about that which matters most.

Divergent Reflections

1. Consider the organizational structure of your congregation. What is it designed to do? Is it designed to create order? Is it designed to encourage creativity? Tell a story about when your congregation changed its organizational structure and the result was a positive change in attitude or behavior.

2. What is one value that your congregation holds that is very important? Consider times when your faith community lived up to that value and also times when it was difficult to act consistently with the value.

3. What was an idea you or someone else had for your church in which the response was, "This will never work"? What happened next? What are some productive actions to take when you hear, "This will never work"?

4. Effective innovation creates results and impact. How does your congregation evaluate the effectiveness of new programs or activities?

Chapter 5
THE PRACTICE OF CONVERSATION

"C onversation is the currency of change," says Gil Rendle, trusted adviser to con-gregations.[1] In many congregations, conversation is not only the currency of change, but also the currency used to connect with God. In some congregations, conversation is the currency for salvation. In others, conversation is the currency for social justice. As a practice, conversation isn't an end unto itself. Conversation is how congregants make meaning of their lives. Through conversation, people address important questions, and those questions build their understanding of who they are, who they want to be, and how they relate to each other. Why am I here? What is the purpose of our life together? Who is my neighbor? How do I respond to an enemy?

The divergent churches we studied give close attention to conversation. Valley and Mountain of Seattle, Washington, encourages radical honesty. Such honesty is required for a person to dive deeply into life's most important issues. At Valley and Mountain listening and radical honesty, elements of the practice of conversation, provide an alternative to focusing on the benign. The leaders write, "It's possible to go through life on the surface of things, securely floating in our little lifeboat where everything seems comfortable and explainable. V&M is like a scuba diving school that helps us get out of the boat and dive deep into the vast, unchartable expanse of the Divine, in whom we live and move and have our being."[2] For divergent churches, the practice of conversation helps participants explore ultimate concerns, discern what matters most in their lives.

As a Christian practice, conversation involves two or more people talking with one another about matters of ultimate concern, in a variety of ways: face to face, in groups, via an Internet chat, in a structured setting, or in a spontaneous manner. In many divergent churches conversation occurs during worship, during small group gatherings, or during Bible study. The practice of conversation also occurs between one person (or a group) and God. In fact, one of the marks of divergent churches is the openness they hold regarding the possibility of hearing an authentic revelation from and with God.

So, conversation exists at the interchange between the human and the Divine, making a way for people to make meaning of their life in relationship to God, family, friends, neighbors, and strangers. Conversation includes words—even an abundance of words. It also includes silence, listening, body language, emotions, inner conversation, and the ability to imagine what another person is thinking. What makes conversation a Christian practice is the extent to which a participant brings to a conversation the ideas, behaviors, traditions, and innovations of the Gospel.

Expanding the Idea of Conversation

Does conversation sound different in a divergent church than it does in a traditional church? It can—more than one divergent church leader uses colorful language to denote a congregation's value to not put up with conversational bull and drivel. Does conversation create different ends or results in a divergent church compared to an established congregation? It is difficult to know. After all, much conversation is private. Conversations take place in quiet offices, over coffee at Starbucks, or during car rides. Many congregational conversations are confidential. Though there are public conversations—sermons, convocations, Facebook posts—many church conversations take place in the sacred space among small groups of people and are not shared beyond those directly involved. So, it is difficult to tell whether conversations in divergent churches are qualitatively different than conversations in other kinds of congregations. Whatever the reality, divergent churches explicitly value conversation. The leaders espouse the value of multilayered, vulnerable, and honest dialogue.

In the divergent churches we studied, three themes regarding conversation and congregational life emerged.

First, *sermons in many divergent churches assume the form of a conversation.* In many settings the sermon is a dialogue between a designated leader and the community. Even when the sermon is not a literal conversation, the sermon is conversational in nature. That is, the rhetoric is informal (though the subject is significant). The preacher invites reflection. Questions are not merely rhetorical. The mode of the sermon is immediate and personal, not distant and objective.

Second, *conversation in divergent churches involves truth-telling.* Conversation is not guarded. It is not superficial. People share what is going on in their lives. Sometimes the sharing is risky, even uncomfortable. Yet, the risk reveals a community that values truth-telling, a community abandoning the mask of self-deception. Divergent congregations personify Luke 12:3: "Whatever you have said in the darkness will be heard in the light, and whatever you have whispered in the rooms deep inside the house will be announced from the rooftops."

Third, *conversation in divergent churches deconstructs (and reconstructs) language about God.* In divergent churches language about God is named, critiqued, and then applied in light of the community's experience. Deconstruction in divergent churches strives for contextual, objective correlation. That is, the word *grace* becomes usable when it evokes an emotion or epiphany through its relationship with a feeling or experience of an individual or community. It's not just the words that count. It's that the words are connected to a life event. Conversation in divergent churches does not attend to remote, three-times-removed life situations. It involves the here and now. When a preacher asks congregants to consider confession of sin (a kind of conversation itself), the participants talk about *their* experience with confession of sin, not something they read about in a book.

All kinds of congregations value conversation. A variety of churches experience the sermon as a conversation, hold honest conversations, and reinterpret long-used theological terms. However, in alternative faith communities, the practice of conversation and these three expressions of the practice are accented with intentionality. In divergent churches, conversation holds the place that preaching, a message proclaimed by a single person occupying the pulpit, did a generation or two ago in established congregations. The activity of offering a message that provides meaning-making is no longer located as the responsibility of one person. In the divergent church, the community's conversation helps participants make sense of God, self, and the world. Sometimes that which has been silent is given voice. In divergent churches, participants use conversation to observe and sometimes rewrite the narrative of their life in relationship with God. So, in this chapter, we examine these three elements of conversation in more detail: the sermon as conversation, the power of truth-telling, and the deconstruction of theological terms.

The Sermon as Conversation

There are many different kinds of sermon. Most forms of sermon involve one person who has been appointed by the faith community (often one with special credentials) to speak a word of God to and for the community. Various forms of sermons include expository sermons, teaching sermons, inductive sermons, story sermons, and so forth.

In many divergent churches, the sermon takes the form of a conversation. Sometimes the sermon is like a conversation even though there is one designated preacher. It is conversational in tone in the way that more than one point of view is given credence. Sometimes the sermon is literally a conversation in which members of small groups talk about scripture or a theological topic.[3]

One divergent church that exemplifies sermon as conversation is Root and Branch of Chicago, Illinois, which is part of the Christian Church (Disciples of Christ). The congregation has two kinds of gatherings. The first and third Sunday mornings include worship at the Gorilla Tango Theatre located near Wicker Park, south of Wrigley Field. The second and fourth Saturdays and Sundays, people are invited to the Welcome Tables, which are dinner church groups that meet in people's homes.

Here is how the leaders of Root and Branch describe their intention: "We want to slow down and pay attention to what matters; other faces in the room, invisible faces in our communities, hidden but real truths that can only emerge with time and care."[4]

Rev. Timothy Kim, a Korean-American, is a pastor at Root and Branch Church. Tim grew up in a conservative church environment but has since moved away from that environment. One of his primary interests as a pastor at Root and Branch is how language about God functions. How deep can a community go? How much honesty about God and humanity can a community hold? At Root and Branch it might be said that talking about the Divine doesn't mean erasing the complicated.[5]

Tim respects the role of the preacher, a person speaking an evocative message to a community. The sermons he preaches aren't dialogue sermons in which the listeners talk during the sermon. They aren't proclamations from high above either. At Root and Branch the sermons are conversational in nature. Congregants have the opportunity to *respond* after the sermon. After the sermon is given, people are invited to share their ideas. Sometimes this sharing continues beyond the time of worship via casual conversation or e-mail exchanges.

It is common for Tim to explore a religious subject, through the sermon, by using real-life examples to illustrate complex ideas. Such rhetoric illumines a subject that might otherwise be abstract or purely cognitive. Tim makes sure the sermon is contextually relevant for the congregants.

Tim says,

> I remember preaching on heaven, basically deconstructing heaven. Instead of ending the sermon by saying, "yes, I hope that heaven is real," I talked about my grandmother who had died. I talked about a documentary I had seen about North Koreans crying about never being able to see their relatives across the country border. I framed this as a theological hope, without using that terminology explicitly or asserting it explicitly. I wanted to share my personal feelings and desires and hopes. I don't know how well this works. But it is my approach at addressing difficult questions.

Think for a moment. Picture what it would be like for you to be sitting with the Root and Branch community ready to hear Tim's sermon on heaven. Do you recall a sermon you've heard about heaven? What could a preacher dare say about heaven? What if heaven doesn't exist? If heaven doesn't exist, does the entire structure of Christianity and congregations collapse? What if heaven does exist? What would it be like to spend eternity with God? How do you get your mind around that idea? Who can say? Who gets to say?

Here's what Tim does: He frames religious concepts so that congregants consider their experience and reason. He doesn't want listeners to accept unexamined concepts. Faith at Root and Branch is held as a self-authoring experience. Someone else shouldn't be writing the story line for you. In this sense, sermons at Root and Branch are biddings for further conversation. The sermon is an invitation to conversation in which one considers their own experience in light of scripture, and theological claims and commitments.

Travel 950 miles due east from Root and Branch, and you'll arrive in Grafton, Massachusetts. In Grafton you can find a feast of sorts almost any Thursday evening. That's because Simple Church, a congregation that started in 2014, is a United Methodist dinner church. Zach Kerzee is the pastor. Zach is committed to simplicity as a spiritual practice. He is interested and involved in organic farming and bread baking. Zach and other leaders of Simple Church state, "Imagine Thanksgiving dinner every week! We meet around a shared meal each Thursday to have conversations that matter. We sing songs. We pray. We laugh. The kids dance. Through our conversations we grow closer to one another, and recognize that all of us are much more connected than we ever imagined."[6]

If you were to walk into the Simple Church gathering after a long drive from Root and Branch, you'd see tables, table cloths, candles; nothing paper, nothing to throw away at the end of the night. You'd smell the bread baking and the soup simmering. At 6:30 p.m. the candles would be lit (beautiful lights dangling from the ceiling).

Participants sing "This Little Light of Mine" as the opening song. Simple Church meets in the fellowship hall of another church building. Simple Church doesn't own a building. To make the temporary space their home (at least for the time of the gathering), the congregation names the place. That is, as part of the liturgy those gathered are encouraged to name what the space is going to be for the group on this evening. Community. Joy. Family. Deep Conversation. Honesty. Life. You've been traveling, remember, so you shout: Rest!

Zach says, "Depending on the group we'll get crazy and beautiful off-the-wall answers. The kids love that part. It's their favorite part, because they can scream it out."

What is the setting for conversation at Simple Church? There is a sequence that helps people prepare for meaningful conversation. Bread is served, the first offering of the Eucharistic meal. Next are the prayers. And then people serve one another food. Soon it is time for the sermon. Zach forms the sermon almost entirely as a conversation. Zach will offer a four-minute reflection that is intended to get conversation going. The topic of conversation is assigned ahead of time. Sometimes the topic has developed from previous discussions. Zach emphasizes that the preconversation talk is only four minutes or so because, as he says,

> The sermon itself is the conversation that we have at the table for thirty minutes. If I went to a dinner party and there is only one guy talking the whole time, that would be weird. And so really what makes a table a table is the fact that everybody who sits at it has an equal place. I call it radically democratic proclamation where we write it together.

On this night the subject for discussion is confession. What was your view of confession as a child? How has it changed? What is the most powerful example of public confession you have witnessed?

The conversation about these questions is the sermon for this evening. You and those with whom you share a table become the authors of the proclamation. What was your view of confession as a child? *I don't think I had one. I knew it was important to apologize but I'm not sure that is the same as confession.* How has it changed? *I worry that I confess too much. I'm too scrupulous. Does God really count every misdeed? I mean, I'm sure I harm someone every day one way or another.* What is the most powerful example of public confession you have witnessed? *Once I was at church, a small country church, and an elder of the congregation stood during the prayer concerns and confessed that he had made a poor decision regarding a financial matter in the church. He was in tears; this eighty-year-old man was in tears.*

Conversations, give and take, listening and asking and coming to terms or not coming to terms with one another—all this is the sermon for the day. But the gathering is not over yet. There is more to come.

The gathering ends with the sharing of juice ("Not wine," as Zach says, "after all, we are a United Methodist church"). The cup representing the forgiveness of sins is shared among the community called Simple Church. There is a child among the other children and adults. She is smiling as she skips from person to person. She has a glass in her hands (remember, no paper, nothing to throw away at the end of the gathering). You are watching her. Soon you hear her. She is touching her glass to everyone's glass, saying, "Cheers."

Everyone drinks after the little girl has touched each person's glass.

Truth-Telling and Testimony

How does conversation in a faith community support truth-telling? We heard many stories from divergent church leaders that demonstrated the value of telling the truth about one's self and telling the truth about the faith community. Divergent churches seek to challenge self-deception and to not make truthfulness a stranger. Let's look at some of the activities that divergent churches have tried in search of authentic speech.

Remember Anne Williamson, whom we met in chapter 3. Anne is the founder and director of WAYfinding in Indianapolis. WAYfinding meets in groups. Over an eight-to-ten-week period (called rounds), the groups explore different practices, themes, issues, and topics. For example, during one round groups explored how to create a sacred table—from the words shared to the food eaten and justice issues around how food is grown. During another the groups explored the enneagram.

One day Anne invited participants to try something new (not unusual with WAYfinding). The assignment was for participants to go to an empty room. What were they to do there? Pray? No. Were they to confess their sins secretly? No. Adapted from Jewish thought, they were to shout at God. Anne had a specific request. Go into the room by yourself and shout at God. Try it. See what happens.

So, you are in a room all by yourself. You have been invited to shout to God, to get it all out, to tell the truth as you know it. What would you shout? It is okay, no one is listening.

God, why did my dad die when I was so young?

You, whoever you are, why do so many suffer?

Lord, I hate the way I've been feeling about him, make it stop!

I don't believe in you and think the notion of talking to you is ridiculous. But speaking my truth aloud feels important.

How much honest speech can a religious community hold? A theme among the divergent churches we studied was appreciation for authentic speech. Actually, it was more than appreciation. It was, in some settings, an immutable aspiration. The Rev. Katie Hays, lead evangelist of Galileo Church in the suburbs of Fort Worth, Texas, named a missional priority of her community as "real relationship, no bullshit, ever." (We learned more about Galileo in our chapter on shaping community.)

Be candid about your questions regarding the Divine. Be authentic about the mistakes you've made. Be open about ways in which you contribute to social injustice. Speak the truth in love. Take risks with your speech. Yes, such honesty will press against cultural expectations. Aspiring to truth telling will create tensions in the church. Yet, the tensions are a welcome alternative to a gathering of false selves. Better to be surprised by honesty than wearied by counterfeit identities. These instructions represent the values that divergent churches bring to the practice of conversation.

Are there boundaries regarding truth-telling? Could one be too honest in a divergent church?

In Anne Tyler's novel *Saint Maybe*, seventeen-year-old Ian has become a wandering soul. A family tragedy has occurred for which he feels responsible. His older brother has died. His sister-in-law has died. And there are three small children who need care. This is not the kind of graduation year that this Presbyterian teenager had expected (the family attends the fictional Dober Street Presbyterian Church in Baltimore).

One night Ian walks the city streets. He comes across a storefront church. The name of the congregation is the Church of the Second Chance (a novelized divergent church?). He has walked in just as the prayers have begun. A mother stands and asks the congregants to remember her son Chuckie, who has just been killed serving in the army. She reminds the congregation that Chuckie was a paratrooper. Somehow, tragically, he jumped from the plane without his parachute. He had forgotten to put on his parachute, the mother says.

Ian thinks to himself: "Could you really forget your parachute?"

Ian pictured one of those animated films where a character strolls off a cliff without noticing and continues strolling in midair, perfectly safe until he happens to look down and then his legs start wheeling madly and he plummets.

He gave a short bark of laughter.

The congregation swiveled and stared at him.[7]

There are social norms about what is appropriate to share about our lives. In divergent churches, the leaders seek to create a culture where vulnerability is honored over pretense. The conversational vulnerability at divergent churches is often what you would commonly expect at a twelve-step group or with a therapist. For someone from a more reserved spiritual tradition experiencing the truth-telling for the first time, such honesty can be challenging. Why would someone share *that*? In some life arenas, vulnerability is experienced as weakness. It can be interpreted as lack of judgment or as neediness. What we are learning is that vulnerability in conversation is part of the search for healthy connection; healthy attachment to people and to the Divine. In the presence of secure attachment, you can be truthful about what you need. You can voice it in conversation. *I need forgiveness. I need attention. I need prayer. I need rest. I need justice. I need a sign from God.* The practice of conversation provides experiences where people seeking meaning and meaningful activities feel secure and understood.

Let's revisit Rev. Timothy Kim and the Root and Branch Church. We've already noted the conversational style of Tim's sermons. Now, let's look at the kind of conversation that takes place at their every-other-week Welcome Table gatherings. Honesty is encouraged and it brings people closer to one another and to God.

Root and Branch hosts two kinds of gatherings. There is the Sunday morning gathering that is their contextualized version of a traditional Sunday worship service. Then on Saturday and Sunday the faith community meets for their Welcome Table experience. These experiences are dinner church groups that meet in people's homes. At Welcome Tables, not only is a meal served (bread and wine is passed), but there are face-to-face conversations too.

If you visit one of the Welcome Tables you will be reminded that everyone doesn't have to agree. Religion can be controversial. The Bible can be controversial. You are invited to bring your questions and opinions. You might observe someone say, "I don't like this passage; it is prejudiced against women." Or someone might say, "This Bible text doesn't depict a God I want to worship." People are encouraged to come to terms with dissimilar viewpoints.

How risky are the discussions? Conversation about religious matters (at the dinner table and elsewhere) involves such subtle nuances as tone of voice, choice of words, diction, body language, pace, silence, and more. Because of so many variables, linguist Deborah Tannen suggests that all conversation misses the mark to a degree. No one can expect to be completely understood. Even among people who know each other well, dialogue entails human limitations. Tannen stresses how all conversation creates a double bind between wanting to connect deeply with another person and wanting to keep distance. The bind with connection is that your own self will be invaded or that you will be invasive toward another. The bind with distance is that it may reveal selfishness or lack of compassion. As Tannen writes, "Because of this double bind, communication will never be perfect; we cannot reach stasis. We have no choice but to keep trying to balance independence with involvement, freedom and safety, the familiar and the strange—continually making adjustments as we list to one side or the other."[8]

No conversation is perfect. No single conversation represents an ideal expression. Non sequiturs are present. People talk after one another quickly and too often there is little direct connection to what has just been stated. Misunderstandings occur. One person says something they regret later. Another withholds something she wishes she had said.

Tim Kim of Root and Branch acknowledges that he occasionally experiences nervousness regarding conversations. If people are talking about issues that matter, then there is the possibility that someone might miss important cues from the group and talk too long or with consideration only for themselves and not for what others have said, so that other people in the conversation lose interest or the feeling of connection. Because of this, Tim and other Root and Branch leaders provide structure for the Welcome Table conversations. Discussions are framed by a story or an experience, a text, or an open-ended question.

The leaders at Root and Branch have developed Holy Ground Rules (to be hospitable to the Holy Spirit) for Welcome Table conversations. The Holy Ground Rules include these covenantal guidelines:

- Give and receive welcome.

- Be present as fully as possible.

- What is offered is by invitation, not demand.

- Speak your truth in ways that respect others' truth.

- Learn to respond to others and yourself with wonder.

- Trust and learn from silence.

- Observe deep confidentiality.

- Leave room for the unexpected to happen.[9]

The Holy Ground Rules provide structure for conversations to convey vulnerability, truth-telling, *and* security.

Truth-Telling and the Cultural Divide

Rev. Jonathan Grace is the campus pastor of Church at the Square in Dallas, Texas. This congregation is supported by Highland Park United Methodist Church, also of Dallas. Highland Park United Methodist is a large congregation and is diverse in different ways. Yet, generally its membership includes middle-class and upper-middle-class households.

By contrast, many of the participants of Church at the Square are homeless neighbors. If you don't have a home, or if in the past you have lived without shelter, you often don't have patience for living with an emotional façade. That mask dropped long ago. You have experienced people who have sympathy for you, but not enough people who recognize your humanity.

So, conversations at Church at the Square testify to struggles, hard-won victories, long nights, rainy days with no roof for protection; this is not the Church of Cheap Grace. It is a congregation abundant with mercy, and the mercy is represented through conversational truth-telling.

Church at the Square has many opportunities for conversation, testimony, and other forms of verbal exchanges. People share joys and concerns during worship. There is no rush. The sharing itself is Sabbath time, a time to linger with what is voiced. On many Sundays, volunteers from other congregations are onsite, often guests from Highland Park United Methodist Church. This means a cultural divide often exists in the worship space, a divide that is bridged by conversation.

After worship, a meal is served. Like many divergent churches, people talk about important things at the dinner table. This is one of the best opportunities for participants at Church at the Square to talk with those from Highland Park. If you could eavesdrop, you might hear conversation about the weather. In this setting, conversation about the weather isn't a disguise to avoid deeper topics. If you've been homeless, you are keenly aware of how the weather can change your life minute to minute.

What other kind of conversations are taking place?

- These two are talking about the struggle of addiction. It may be the first time a member of Highland Park shares about his son's struggles in a church setting.

- These four are talking about leads they have regarding housing. A volunteer listens respectfully offering a word of encouragement.

- This person is talking to a volunteer about their health (homeless people are often compromised physically). The volunteer feels free to share about her own health challenges.

The practice of conversation at Church of the Square provides the opportunity for people to hold a mirror to one another. Rich and poor, homeless and housed— yes, there are significant cultural differences. Yet, there is *some* common humanity reflected back to one another as people talk with one another. *This divergent church experience brings about convergence.*

Neuroscientists have identified a reality called mirror neurons. A mirror neuron is a brain cell that exchanges information through electrical and chemical signals.

Mirror neurons are sensitive neurons. That is, they help you feel what another person is feeling. They nudge you to imitate what you observe another person doing. Have you noticed how, if a person near you yawns, you may automatically yawn too? Your mirror neurons are at work. As Daniel Siegel writes, via mirror neurons, "We not only imitate others' behaviors but actually come to resonate with their feelings—the internal mental flow of their minds."[10]

In divergent churches mirror neurons seem particularly active. At least that is one way to put it. Another way to put it is that congregations like Church at the Square are forming people of faith to be empathetic, to be willing to internalize what life is like for another. You don't talk about things as much as you are talking (what would be the best preposition?) *in* things. God is present in the space between people.

It is Easter. Over sixty volunteers from Highland Park United Methodist Church are present at Church at the Square. During the sharing of joys and concerns, one of the homeless neighbors says it is the two-year anniversary of her baby passing away. At many a congregation it would be considered (somehow understandably) beyond a cultural norm to testify of personal grief on the day of resurrection. It feels awkward for a moment. Yet, it is clear that people hear her. They pray for and with her. There is a connection made in the moment. The community is able to hold the still real grief of the mother (how could it be any other way?) while also celebrating the resurrection of Jesus Christ.

Attunement and attachment change the structure of the brain. *In divergent churches, conversations change the commitments of the faith community.*

Deconstruction of Conversational Language

Many of the divergent church clergy talked about deconstruction, particularly deconstruction of Christian language. Faith language holds multiple meanings. You cannot assume that the word *grace* has shared meaning for congregants. Just as divergent churches are reinventing what it means to be church, divergent churches are reinventing what religious words mean.

Most divergent church clergy we talked to deconstruct religious language in a way that leads to new construction. Ideas from the old structure aren't completely discarded. Yet, new meanings are sketched like an architect's conceptual drawings.

For example, the word is imagined as a first draft of an ancient idea. It is not so much explained as it is explored, usually with personal experiences. The word might not resonate with certain participants. Some attempt is made to put the structure of grace back together so that the word still functions for the faith community, based on how the community has talked about the word. For divergent churches, deconstruction is not the final act. It is like the church is engaged in experiential word study on any number of religious words: *grace, salvation, Christ, church, forgiveness, confession,* and so forth. Yet, the conversation isn't an academic deep dive into Hebrew or Greek. It is an exploration of how these words function in the here and now, in English, in the lives of those who are gathered.

Remember Rev. Timothy Kim from the Root and Branch Church of Chicago. Tim is attentive to the use of theological language in conversation. He has reconstructed faith language in his own life as he has moved personally from a more conservative religious worldview to a more progressive understanding. At Root and Branch there is not shared vocabulary of Christian concepts, though Tim does think a shared vocabulary is important. It's that a shared vocabulary is not possible at this point in the congregation. So many who participate at Root and Branch are young adults between the ages of twenty-one and thirty-five. Many of them do not have experience with the Christian vocabulary. Plus, many of them are okay with a degree of unsettledness when it comes to words and meanings. Not every word has to be defined in some standard or right way.

At Root and Branch, like so many divergent churches, people have different views of what religion is, and what falls within the boundaries of religious experience. These different views are expressed not only through practices but through language, sometimes a combination of both. At a Root and Branch retreat, the focus was on prayer. One person at the retreat said, "I'm an atheist. I don't have any belief in God." The person went on to say, "I'm interested in prayer as a way for me to connect spiritually with myself, the world, and the universe, but I don't have a sense of praying to God." Tim notes that, at Root and Branch, a person holding this view could find a place in the community because the congregation doesn't project normative claims and assertions onto participants.

Religious deconstructionist John Caputo distinguishes "particular beliefs from an underlying faith and hope in life itself."[11] This hope against hope requires a stance of deconstruction. Faith, atheism, and agnosticism can no longer be categorically contained. What emerges is an unnerving religion that exists, in tension with, yet alongside a more comforting religion.[12]

Congregations like Root and Branch dare to rethink the norms for faith and reason. And the dare exists in conversation between people.

So, what does this deconstruction sound like? We asked Tim to say more about how deconstructed faith language works at Root and Branch. He responded,

> It would be uncommon in our church for me to get up and say something like "God's grace saved us all." I could say that sentence but then I would deconstruct it. One tricky aspect is that you can't be deconstructing all the time. There would be no foundation for us to stand on. Being willing to enter into relationships of questioning; asking about and sharing ideas is essential. Our goal isn't simply deconstructing.

There is some sense of putting these things back together again. The putting back together again happens through stories. I can share an aspect of the subject at hand and why it is important to me personally, which invites people to be drawn into the concept being considered without it feeling mandatory.

In divergent churches like Root and Branch, dinner table conversations about scripture and life are not zero-sum experiences. Insight received by one does not represent a loss for another. There is more to share. There is more to say. At Root and Branch and other divergent congregations where learning is connected to conversation, there is a *to be continued* dynamic to discussion. The *to be continued* dynamic acknowledges that human discourse is complex. Conversation is precarious. Human beings do not always say what they mean, or mean what they say. Listeners do not hear the speaker's meaning as the speaker intended.

Religious terms—whether it be heaven, hell, grace, salvation, or any term important to you—are employed "along the way" (as opposed to as a destination) because of the tentative nature of all conversation. There is rarely sufficient time or wisdom to consider a discussion a closed deal. There are rarely sufficient voices or points of view represented to say that a particular commitment is the final word. Religious coming to terms are expressions of ongoing considerations. There may be limits to answers. Yet, in divergent churches, there is an abundance of conversation, of important matters being open for discussion, for conversations about meaning-making to be in unlimited supply.

The question "What do we make of heaven?" does not have to be settled once and for all. It cannot be settled once and for all.

Healthy relationships are essential to a faith community deconstructing terms of belief. Participants who flourish in such settings are those who are able to be in the same room with others who differ greatly from them and not be overly anxious or defensive. Participants who flourish in such settings have tolerance for ambiguity. They are able to attune to what others are saying in a way that creates empathy, not judgment. Conversation is a practice that results in regard for one another and connection to the Creator.

In his book *Telling Secrets*, Frederick Buechner offers a critique of the church as he has experienced it. He is comparing the church to twelve-step groups. He looks around at the people in the group and he remembers, "Know that you can trust these people with your secrets because they have trusted you with theirs."[13] He writes,

> I believe that the church has an enormous amount to learn from them. I also believe that what goes on in them is far closer to what Christ meant his church to be, and what it originally was, than much of what goes on in most churches I know. These groups have no buildings or official leadership or money. They have no rummage

sales, no altar guilds, no every-member canvases. They have no preachers, no choirs, no liturgy, no real estate. They have no creeds. They have no program. They make you wonder if the best thing that could happen to many a church might not be to have its building burn down and to lose all its money. Then all that the people would have left would be God and each other.[14]

One way in which divergent churches seek to represent Christ and create the community he intended is through conversation. It is through honest conversation that the participants experience God and risk being an authentic self with others. The practice of conversation takes place as part of the sermon, in moments of truth-telling and while religious terms are deconstructed so as to hold authentic meaning in the church's life together.

Conversation is one form of communication in divergent churches. Another form is artistic expression. Divergent churches use the arts to find meaning and to represent the impact of the Gospel in everyday life. In the next chapter we look at the practice of artistic expression in divergent churches.

Divergent Reflections

1. How and where do the most meaningful conversations in your congregation take place? Who is involved? What is the subject matter?

2. What do you think of the assertion that all conversation misses the mark to some degree? What do you do to create the conditions for healthy conversations in your church and in your life?

3. What words of faith would you like to deconstruct? That is, what words of faith have become empty in your faith community? How might you recover the power of these particular words?

4. What conversations haven't been resolved in your church? How might you continue these conversations in healthy ways?

Chapter 6
THE PRACTICE OF ARTISTIC EXPRESSION

This chapter is about the practice of artistic expression. The religious practice of artistic expression involves creative activities like music, drama, painting, craft making, and more as a way to explore the faith claims and commitments of a worshiping community. In the churches we learned from, artistic expression helps one understand scripture and life. Artistic expression is a way to draw on the gifts of participants to strengthen the church. It is for something deeper too, something less institutional. Artistic expression in the context of divergent churches is a way to express one's yearnings, joys, doubts, and hopes. Participants in divergent churches use art to explore life and faith.

In this chapter, we will explore the specific practice of artistic expression as it plays out in two divergent churches: Convergence and Wild Goose Christian Community.

Convergence: Making Art to Explore the Spirit

Often our understanding of the arts in church is limited to the choir, or the beauty of stained glass, and maybe a few children's theatrical or musical activities. Artistic expression is something that happens as part of an occasional program or activity. But at Convergence, a divergent church in Alexandria, Virginia, art intersects with all aspects of their congregational life—worship, shaping community, leadership, community engagement, and spiritual formation. Artistic expression is a way of life. The people of Convergence create and experience art as integral to spiritual formation and theological discourse. Artistic expression and interpretation are the means by which the people at Convergence practice their spirituality and explore biblical and theological concepts. So, artistic expression is itself a practice.

At Convergence, activities related to artistic expression match the definition of practice we stated in chapter 3: *Religious (artistic) practices are contextualized expressions of essential activities done by people who seek to thoughtfully and competently embody their religious commitments with and for others.*

The leaders of Convergence state, "We believe the artist's imagination and rich interior life are of great value. We foster an environment where this is nurtured."[1] This appreciation of the artistic imagination has been shared by people of faith through the centuries. Those representing the Valparaiso University Project on Education and Formation of People in Faith observe the power of singing as artistic expression. Their observations apply to all kinds of artistic expression:

> What we sing and how we sing [and the music we play, the art we create] reveals much of who we are, and entering into another's song and music making [art] provides a gateway into their world, which might be much different from our own. Something is shared in singing that goes beyond the words alone. This something has taken shape over many centuries in a practice that expresses our deepest yearning and dearest joy.[2]

Whether one is painting an image from scripture, or creating a drama from a parable, or singing a traditional folk song on banjo, human experiences of yearning and joy are expressed. These expressions are not about mundane matters. Creative representations, whether they are drama or music or painting, depict the desire to be more closely related to the work of God in the world. Artistic expression is a way to explore existential commitments related to essential matters like the presence (or absence) of God, belonging, forgiveness, and much more.

What would it be like to be part of a congregation that uses art all the time to represent the most engaging realities of life? Convergence is a community of people who not only value creativity, they see it as inseparable from spirituality. They believe that imagination, creativity, and the arts are spiritual matters and their cultivation is of benefit to the church, the local community, and the world. Convergence consistently creates opportunities for artistic expression to represent its religious claims and commitments. Let's look more closely at how Convergence developed and the particular ways in which artistic expression is essential to this divergent church.

The Evolution of Convergence and a Pastor's Roots in Theatre

Lisa Cole Smith, the pastor and artistic director of Convergence, has a background in theatre as an actor and director. She attended seminary to dig deeper into her relationship with God and to try to find a way to meld the worlds of art and faith for herself. She found permission to explore the dynamic connection between art and faith in seminary and was given the opportunity to explore the ways they might practically inform one another. As she was preparing to graduate, she planned to continue her work with the theatre company she founded while in school. Working with local professional actors, she produced plays that had deeper human relevancy, exploring questions about God, meaning, and life: Why do bad things happen? Where is God in the midst of such bad things? How should we relate as human beings, given our differences? Where does the strength of the human spirit come from? The theatre company regularly engaged in conversation as a cast. They held talkback sessions after each play. It was a fruitful experience that Lisa planned to continue.

But as she was graduating from seminary she was approached by the trustees of a sixty-year-old Baptist church in Alexandria, Virginia, looking to restart. They had seed money, a time frame of five years, and a desire to try something different as a church. The group needed a leader. So, they asked Lisa, "What would you do with this space?" She put together a proposal built around the idea of being a resource center for the local artistic community. One of those resources would eventually be a church that would grow out of the artistic resource center. So, the idea of an artistic community in some ways predated the idea of a new church community. Like other divergent churches, it is not unusual for the faith community to develop out of the activity that provides meaning. The existential desire to explore meaning through theatre (and other arts) invigorated ideas for the new community. The development of Convergence as a worshiping community developed from the yearning to connect spirituality through the arts.

So Convergence began in 2007. According to Lisa, there has been a lot of experimentation to discern how the arts and faith can intersect more intentionally. Like many divergent church leaders, Lisa experienced and observed that something was missing in the church world. In the church, she experienced a lack of imagination, creativity, fullness of religious practice, and even of a fullness of community. In the theatre, she had a rich community and had spiritual experiences with God through art-making that were often far more potent than what she experienced in church. This was frustrating and sad. What was missing in church? Something needed to be done to bring these two into active conversation. Hence her proposal: an experiment to bring these worlds together.

Professor Deborah Haynes informs Lisa's thinking about this experiment. Haynes talks about finding artists who might accept the call to be prophetic critics and imaginative visionaries in the world. Because of their interior worlds and capacity to make insights, artists are positioned to see the state of where we are, are hopeful (or honest) about the future, and possess the skills to paint a vision for what could be.[3] Lisa sees people within the artistic world who are picking up this spiritual questioning but who don't have a community where that exploration is welcomed and fed. She also knew that, at the same time, many in the wider church were feeling frustrated and limited, not knowing how to connect their search for God with their creative gifts.

Convergence developed as a hybrid. It is a community arts center and church. It provides opportunities for artistic and spiritual development. If you are part of Convergence you might participate in activities consistent with many other faith communities. You might worship on Sunday, participate in Bible study and discipleship groups, sing at Taizé prayer services, and attend faith gatherings—familiar building blocks of Christian faith and practice even if the forms and expression are slightly unfamiliar. Where Convergence most distinctly diverges from the practices of the congregation that formerly met at its location, are the opportunities for creative development. All throughout the year there are art classes, open mic events, and activities in artist studios. There are opportunities to meet artists in residence, contribute to an arts incubator, and participate in art exhibits. This is an overview of Convergence. Let's look at a particular experience at Convergence that represents the practice of artistic expression and the positive energy it provides this divergent faith community.

Improvisation as Spiritual Practice

This story is of two Convergence members, Dan and Kathy. Dan, a skeptic of organized religion, arrives at Convergence as a creator and host of the local punk, do-it-yourself house show scene in the northern Virginia area. As musician and producer, he mentors and builds community for kids in the punk scene who don't have any place to meet. After several years, Dan joins the Convergence staff to bring his community-building skills to the larger project and decides that as part of his new job, he will attend the Sunday night church services to understand all facets of life at Convergence.

Kathy, on the other hand, has always had a deep spiritual life and has been a longtime Christian and member of a church. She's had occasional negative church experiences. Kathy asks a lot of questions. She is a lifelong learner when it comes to the experience of God. Kathy's willingness to speak up, share her experience, and ask questions is a positive force in Convergence. Her curiosity fits Convergence's culture of encouraging imaginative visionaries (remember Professor Haynes's observations). She begins participating in Convergence around the same time Dan starts attending Sunday services.

During Lent the congregation studies the story in Luke 7 in which Jesus has dinner at Simon the Pharisee's house and the sinful woman washes Jesus's feet. During the interactive Bible study (part of their normal Sunday service) they read the story aloud and discuss the passage. The gathering takes place in their theatre space where the resident theatre company has built the seedy hotel room set for the play *Fool for Love*. This particular backdrop grounds their worship in the context of the everyday.

As part of this service they look at a series of paintings about the biblical story. They explore who is depicted in each painting, how each artist has arranged the people, and what that says about the interpretation of the story. In some paintings, Jesus appears to not pay any attention to the woman at all, instead focusing on his host and other guests. In some, he compassionately reaches out to the woman at his feet. In many of the paintings, there are different people present both far away from everything that's happening as well as close by, huddled near Jesus. The group looks at one painting in which the gathering with Jesus is in the background. In the foreground is a woman, presumably a kitchen worker, represented in a pensive, reflective posture doing her work. What is it like to be at the outer perimeter of a great event? Such is the question of the prophetic visionaries in our midst.

The congregation is also asked to consider, "Which painting speaks to you? Where would you be in that painting?" There's talk about the posture of those depicted. There's conversation about the various ways the woman is illustrated and what these different images say about the story and the relationship between Jesus and the woman.

After examining several paintings of this story, they begin an improvisation game. Note: this is at the soul of what Convergence does, integrating the spiritual with artistic expression. Those at the gathering follow three basic rules of improvisation: say the first thing that comes to mind, make your partner look good, and say "yes, and"—accept all invitations. These rules of improvisation infuse Convergence's identity. The rules serve not only as rules of improvisation but also as rules of community; how they engage with each other and with the wider community; how they create space for deeper engagement of scripture and of theological principles.

To conclude this worship and study time Lisa leads the group through some warm-up activities, and then the improvisation work (or is it play?) begins as participants create their own image of the biblical story. The scene needs to be populated with volunteers from the congregation. The group is asked to decide who needs to be in the picture. First on the list is Jesus. Lisa asks for a volunteer. She waits. No one responds. Until, that is, Kathy hesitantly agrees. "Okay, I'll be Jesus." Kathy would feel much more comfortable as the woman washing Jesus's feet, but she is willing to put herself out there for the sake of the group exercise.

Even in a highly creative community like Convergence people can be reluctant to try something outside their comfort zone. Not everyone at Convergence is an artist, and even those who make some form of art won't necessarily feel comfortable practicing a different discipline. But this edge of discomfort is exactly where interesting things start to happen as people stretch their limits and become open to new insights through unique experiences. Having a naturally curious and adventurous person like Kathy present provides energy for others to feel safe to experiment with their own creativity. So it is significant that Kathy is present at this particular point in time when a certain group of people are together. She is ready to improvise, which helps others be willing to play along. Yes, there is an element of play to all of this.

Kathy walks up to the front of the space because the group decides that she should be in the center of their picture.

Next up is the woman who washes Jesus's feet. "Who should we have?" asks Lisa.

This time, a hand goes up immediately. It is Dan. "I'll do it," he says. The group decides to place him sitting on the ground at Kathy's feet, and they lock eyes.

One by one everyone within the congregation willing to participate finds a character and a place on the stage to create their own scene of the dinner at Simon the Pharisee's house.

As the group settles into their poses on stage, Lisa asks them to freeze, and after a period of silence she asks them to find one line of dialogue to say aloud. "What's going through your head?" she asks. "What are you thinking or feeling as your character in this moment right now, where this woman has just started washing Jesus's feet?" There is an immediacy in the room. Can you feel it? This is happening right here, right now.

Lisa moves among the group positioned on the stage and touches each person one at a time on the shoulder, cueing them to say aloud their thoughts.

Moving from the periphery of the group inward, she touches one fellow on the shoulder. He has his iPhone out. He's texting to someone in the group: "Hey Cheryl, what are you doing after this?"

The next person Lisa taps says the line, "What's for dinner? I'm hungry." Someone else peeking through a half-open doorway (remember this takes place on a theatre set) says, "I don't know if I belong here."

A young woman who sees herself in a subservient role bows down. She says, "That should be me," in reference to the woman washing Jesus's feet with her hair. When tapped on their shoulders, those playing the part of Jesus's followers say things like, "What's he going to do?" and "What if this is really inappropriate?" Lisa ultimately makes her way to Jesus and the woman, that is, Kathy and Dan, the spiritual learner and the punk band promoter. They have been locked in a gaze for minutes. By now they both have tears in their eyes. Something is happening between them.

Lisa touches Dan on the shoulder. He looks straight at Kathy (Jesus) and says, "Thank you."

Lisa touches Kathy on the shoulder and Kathy says to Dan, "You moved me." At this moment, Lisa experiences the room being electrified. "Something just happened," she says. "It's as if we are in this story. Now."

Art and Faith Converging

This story represents how the practice of artistic expression provides opportunities to interpret experiences of faith and life. It also invites observations about interpretation in divergent churches. Consider Rembrandt's painting *Return of the Prodigal Son*. In the painting, the father's hands are on the prodigal son's shoulder and upper back. What are the hands doing? Are they giving a blessing? Are they comforting? Are they pulling the son close? Are the hands pressing firmly or lightly? Are the hands warm or cool? Making meaning out of those hands is fun and engaging. There's no answer because no one can ask Rembrandt. And who knows? Maybe Rembrandt was just trying to draw the most lifelike hands he could draw. But we are free to interpret. We are drawn to engage the art, to experience it on a deeper and multifaceted level. The responsibility of response is given to us, and the act of response is itself a form of artistic expression. *In divergent churches, meaning-making as it occurs through a variety of practices is given to the community to discern.*

At Convergence, interpretation and subsequent meaning-making occur through artistic expression. We have experienced this as a unique element of divergent churches. In more established congregations it is often, depending on the polity of the church, decision making about the church that is collaborative; that is, decision making about strategies and operations are given to members as part of their work as members. Some, maybe many, of the divergent churches we learned from were not highly collaborative when it came to shaping community or making institutional decisions. Often there was a small guiding group or the lead clergy held the vision and made operational decisions. However, concerning matters of meaning-making and interpretation of faith, the divergent churches become egalitarian. The more voices the better. Your expression, your interpretation is valid.

In the world of religion and spirituality, we often try to stake our claim in certain schools of thought. I'm progressive. You are evangelical. She finds comfort in the immanence of God. He seeks transcendence. Like other spheres of life, church life is often exemplified by categorical thinking. We attach ourselves to groupings and classifications. The danger is that the grouping or classification becomes who we are. Expressing spirituality and faith through artistic interpretation reminds us that there is room to experience and interpret deep truth anew, sometimes beyond categories. Fresh interpretation is rooted in the present, in the here and now of any given moment. The people of Convergence engaged in fresh interpretation when they reenacted the anointing of Jesus's feet.

Then we're back on the set of *Fool for Love* with the people of Convergence.

"What would you say?" asks Lisa.

When Dan said, "Thank you," Lisa thought, *Of course. Of course that's what you'd say!*

And then she reflects that if she were acting as Jesus, she would probably have responded to "thank you" with "you're welcome, my child" or something else that sounds gracious and holy.

But Kathy's response of "You moved me" is unexpected. It is raw and real, and it rings true. It is as if the exchange between Jesus and the woman has time-traveled into the experience between Dan and Kathy.

Lisa offers to the group what she is noticing from experience. Jesus is indeed moved by the people he encounters. He is moved to respond with justice, love, compassion, empathy, anger. It is through reenactment and reflection that the people of Convergence bring their faith to life by practicing artistic expression.

More conversations follow.

The man peeking in the doorway asks, "I've heard people talk about *experiencing* God before, but I've never had that happen. Is that what just happened?"

Dan comments, "I had to be that woman because I knew exactly how she felt. Some people were asking why she was crying. But I felt like, of course she was crying because what other response would you have in that situation?"

And for Kathy, her line "You moved me" was inspired by Dan's simple "thank you" response. She identifies with his expression of gratitude. But when she spun the point of view to see the situation as Jesus might have, she knew deep in herself the natural response to the woman, to anyone in need. She was moved as Jesus might have been.

That simple "Thank you. . . . You moved me" exchange was a representative example of how Convergence is still developing as a group of individuals into a congregation. There were several new people there that day. The reenactment experience created a sense of immediacy to God and closeness to one another. It isn't enough for a church to declare the desire to be prophetic critics and imaginative visionaries. It is more essential for the community to experience being prophetic critics and imaginative visionaries. In this experience, the Bible story was not just about something that happened in the past. The story became something that was happening to all of them in that moment. It represents the core of Convergence, the place where artistic and spiritual identities meet and are celebrated.

A practice entails doing something repeatedly. This repetition helps the practitioner build internal muscle that provides access to something new within the self. The practitioner develops a habit or familiarity with thoughts and movements that give him or her access to a channel that taps into something bigger than herself or himself. When the practitioner seeks connection with the Divine, their practice is a spiritual practice.

We've explored drama and improvisation in terms of the practice of artistic expression. Let's turn our attention to another divergent church that immerses itself in another kind of artistic expression: Appalachian culture, including the music of the Appalachian people.

Finding Common Ground in Appalachian Music

Music is central to the Wild Goose congregation. Music is the holy other that shapes this divergent church. Wild Goose is a worshiping community. It is Christ-centered. It is connected to the Presbyterian Church (USA). In addition to these facts, the essence of this divergent church is its honoring of Appalachian culture, particularly the music of Appalachia.

Rev. Edwin Lacy, founding pastor of Wild Goose, knows and plays traditional Appalachian music, music with deep roots in Floyd County, Virginia. The music is a bridge for seemingly unrelated people. Mountain farmers have been in Floyd County for generations. In the 1970s, hippies moved into Floyd County because they loved the green, rolling landscape and quiet mornings. They loved the fact that it was away from the noise of the city. It didn't hurt that land was relatively inexpensive. The hippies loved the mountain culture. They loved the crafts. They loved the old-time ways of doing things, and, more than anything, they loved the music.

Imagine the contrast between the hippies and the deep-rooted farmers of Floyd County. The hippies had long hair and wore funny clothes and didn't "live like they should." But music was the conduit that helped the old farmers and the hippies begin building relationships. The hippies asked the farmers to teach them how to play old-time banjo and the fiddle. They wanted to learn the old songs. These requests softened the hearts of the mountain farmers. And so, a beautiful relationship between them grew. They each kept their own identity, but they began to have real community. A lot of those farmers now farm with organic methods because they learned them from the hippies. Over the decades, the divisions between the two groups have decreased and the major contributing factor is music.

When Edwin started Wild Goose, he wanted the worshiping community to reflect this unique history. As a seasoned Appalachian musician, he knew that the music was going to be central to the church. Edwin recruited several of his local musician friends to play at the church. But over the initial weeks those musicians came and went, sometimes leaving Edwin as the sole musician at church. Edwin said, "A solo banjo player wasn't going to fit the bill." He needed more and consistent musicians. That's when internationally renowned Appalachian musician Mac Traynham came in. He arrived one Tuesday with his fiddle and his guitar and he played a little. Then the next week, he and Edwin played together. As the weeks passed, Mac invited other musicians to church. Pretty soon, they had a trio, and then a quartet, and then a little band. Soon thereafter, Mac, not Edwin, suggested certain songs to play during the worship service. Little by little, Mac, without ever having a conversation with Edwin, became the Wild Goose music leader. That's how things work in the Appalachian culture. That which is good and right and true unfolds naturally, like the melody of a folk tune.

This progression set the tone for how the church community was going to develop. "It was going to be Spirit led," says Edwin. It was going to be organic. It was going to be participatory. It was going to be ultra-inclusive. Other elements of the church's life started to reflect this same tone. The meal that was initially catered during the first few weeks of gathering quickly became a potluck. People hung curtains around the church without being told. People volunteered to lead the discussion around scripture.

This organic development mirrored a deep Appalachian tradition. For instance, when music is passed down from the farmers to the hippies, or from a father to his daughter, no committees are formed to talk about how this is going to happen. It just happens. It's a very natural oral tradition and organic process. And just as what happens when people get together to play old-time music, there aren't musical scores about who's going to do what. People intuitively know what to play. One person will play the melody for the first round of the song and then he or she will pass it on to the next one and play something supportive. There's never a spoken word about this process. It's beautiful, natural, and organic. The give and take builds community. If you are present you realize that there are times when you have to let the music sing on its own (at least it feels that way) and let God sing God's song. During the songs it is as if God is guiding the whole experience. It is a glimpse of what living one's whole life in the providential care of God is like. At least that is what the artistic expression of music teaches at Wild Goose.

Edwin says, "It changes everything about how we do all our practices, how we eat together, how we practice hospitality and so forth."

And so it goes at Wild Goose. The practice of artistic expression through music parallels the key values by which the community is shaped: organic, improvised, home-grown, rooted in the mountains. Christ may have journeyed through Palestine, but his spirit takes shape in Appalachia too.

"Everything we do celebrates Appalachian culture in some small way," says Edwin.

What are the marks of Appalachian culture? Edwin says, "The music, of course, also homemade crafts including quilting and building furniture. Storytelling too. A strong sense of independence and self-sufficiency balanced by deep caring for neighbors in need."

At first Wild Goose was known as the square-dancing church. After worship on Tuesday nights, participants would push back the rocking chairs and turn the sanctuary into a dance floor. Now the square dance nights are four times a year or so.

Worship has become the primary focus of the community, and, yes, the worship has a distinctly Appalachian flavor.

They serve communion out of a Mason jar. Fiddle, mandolin, and banjos anchor the music. A fireplace sits where the pulpit used to be. Quilts adorn the walls. When the church took possession of its building, they took out the pews and put in a circle of rocking chairs. In the middle of that circle, you can see the light and dark spots where the floor has faded around the outline of the pews. They keep the floor that way because they want to remember that creating Wild Goose Christian Community is built on the shadows and imprints of the generations of people who went before them.

If you visit worship, you might be there on a Tuesday when Edwin and the other musicians begin to play a song. It begins with the plaintive tones of Edwin's banjo playing clawhammer style (the thumb beats the rhythm; two other fingers pick or flick the melody). The song may be new to you, so listen to its message:

Gone, gonna rise again.

And we dug his grave on the mountainside.[4]

The lyrics tell of livestock, a corn crib, and ham in the smokehouse. The resident didn't have much but worked hard in life. He's gone now. That's true. It's also true that he is going to rise again.

The resurrection theme of the song fits Wild Goose. After all, the community meets in a Presbyterian church building that was previously closed. The congregation seeks to raise up the best traditions of their culture so the customs don't die in an urban-oriented United States. This is a community that trusts the power of the risen Christ. The whole countryside and its inhabitants, someday, might just be gone, but in Christ it is gonna rise again.

The music at Wild Goose is more innovative and diverse than you might think. Certainly the emphasis is on bluegrass and other Appalachian forms. Yet, the community sings hymns and responses. To Edwin's ears the Doxology sounds sad when played slowly on a church organ. And it isn't meant to be a sad song. It is a praise song. Edwin observes that when you play it on a banjo, it brightens right up. Add a mandolin and it works quite well. At Wild Goose the practice of artistic expression means taking certain songs and changing them and claiming them for the community. This involves creativity. It involves the same kind of imagination that theatrical improvisation requires.

With the dramatic representation of scripture at Convergence and the making of Appalachian music at Wild Goose, artistic expression is integral to the religious experience. Yes, art exists (thankfully) in all realms of life, not just the explicitly religious.

Yet, in these two divergent churches the human, artistic impulse reveals theological realities like thanksgiving, emotional connection, resurrection, and praise. Whether you create something that never existed (*creation ex nihilo*) or adapt something from a text or a tradition (making meaning from improvisation) you bear witness to the ultimate source and composition of life. The very act of artistic expression is to participate in co-creation with the Creator.

These two churches, Convergence and Wild Goose, engage the practice of artistic expression through drama and music. These activities express dearest yearnings and deep joys. They help participants make meaning. These activities build a sense of community. In the next chapter, we'll get to know more congregations and how rich connections are maintained. We'll move from the theatre and the sound of the banjo to the dinner table. We'll see how divergent churches shape their congregational community in refreshing and unconventional ways through breaking bread together.

Divergent Reflections

1. If your congregation was going to collaborate with an arts group, what group would that be? What factors might go into making this a healthy collaboration?

2. Make a list of various aspects of artistic expression that are evident in your congregation. Which one of these is most consistent with the values of your church and truest to your geographic location? How often do you make this particular practice accessible to more people?

3. Can secular artistic expression be a spiritual practice? How does non-religious art and music inform your congregation's life? And how does religious creative expression from your congregation inform your wider community, your religious life, and vice versa?

4. Let's combine two practices: shaping community and artistic expression. How might artistic expression be used in a board, council, committee, or team meeting to support good conversation and sound discernment?

Chapter 7
THE PRACTICE OF BREAKING BREAD

A church started hosting fellowship hour after worship. Members served donuts and coffee. You'd see seven-year-olds walking quickly away from tables juggling five (maybe six) donut holes. At some point the donuts and coffee were replaced with members taking turns serving other kinds of snacks. One week a family would prepare chips, salsa, and guacamole dip. The next week, another family would serve various kinds of fruit—strawberries, blueberries, and melons. Soon the snacks were replaced with full meals. After worship people would stride into the fellowship hall and discover chili ready to be served, or hotdogs and baked beans, or a variety of small plate offerings of food from South Korea. People talked about the week that was and the week to come. They'd linger. Several stayed to clean up.

Have you ever noticed that our fellowship time lasts longer than our worship time?

Eating together is a universal human activity. So it goes that congregations of all kinds experience meals together.

Eating together goes by many names in the Christian tradition. As described by Paul in 1 Corinthians 11, early Christian communities shared a meal together. At some point this shared meal became more ritualized. It became the sacrament of communion, known also as the Lord's Supper, or Holy Communion, or the Eucharist. In addition to a sacramental meal, churches of all kinds share common meals: potlucks, pitch-ins, love feasts, or fellowship meals.

We have chosen to call the experience of eating together in divergent churches the practice of breaking bread. The phrase "breaking bread" is both literal and metaphorical. In most divergent churches, eating together includes the Lord's Supper every week. This sacrament contains the ritual breaking of the loaf of bread. In divergent churches "breaking bread" also denotes a number of other activities: fellowship meals, growing food, baking bread, selling food, gathering people in spaces like bars and restaurants, and much more.

What makes such occasions a practice is the universality of these activities and religious intentionality involved in preparing, serving, blessing, and sharing the meal or the bread or the produce. The intentionality facilitates a connection between the people participating in the meal and the Divine's role in the shared meal. If a group of people regularly prepares and eats a meal with mindfulness and intentionality, over time the people grow closer together. When people break bread in congregations, more than nourishment is occurring. The food becomes a renewable symbol of assimilating the presence of God into one's self and into the community.

How is breaking bread different in divergent churches than in more established congregations? In divergent churches we noticed how mealtime is integrated with worship. Depending on the setting, it is difficult to tell the difference between the sacrament of communion and a fellowship dinner.

In divergent churches the people who break bread together embody the words of the Protestant communion liturgy: "This is the joyful feast of the Lord." Many of us have been to worship services where the words "joyful feast" don't match the reality. The communion bread is stale, not homemade. The music is dour. Serving the meal is excruciatingly slow. Yet, at divergent churches the sacrament is a celebration. People smile. The music is celebratory or, if not celebratory, then soulful.

It isn't unusual for divergent churches to embrace the values of the farm-to-table movement, preferring direct acquisition of the food from the producer. Sometimes the meals at divergent churches are made up of fruits and vegetables grown by those participating in the life of the congregation.

At divergent churches breaking bread together is a sign of God's realm—the rich and the poor eating together, for example. In established churches those who have access to more resources might be serving a meal to the poor. (This is not a bad thing; charity is sometimes a necessary good.) In divergent churches those with resources and those without are sharing meals *with* one another. It is an egalitarian affair.

In fact, every divergent church we learned from (with one exception) hosts a meal that is integrated into the rhythm of its weekly gathering. The Cowboy Church has breakfast. Church at the Square eats immediately after worship. Root and Branch hosts their Welcome Tables. So it goes that the practice of breaking bread isn't scheduled like a quarterly potluck at an established Main Street church. The practice of breaking bread occurs almost every time these divergent churches gather. What does a family do together? They sit down and eat. What does a divergent church do together? The participants sit down and eat. How does Acts 2:46 go? "Every day, they met together in the temple and ate in their homes. They shared food with gladness and simplicity."

Two congregations we learned from are examples of the robust activities that make up the practice of breaking bread together in divergent churches: Simple Church in Grafton, Massachusetts, and The Garden Church in San Pedro, California. Both of these churches are examples of divergent churches that make the entire worship service an expanded communion meal. Instead of communion being one part of the worship service, the whole service is the assimilation of the elements of food, wine, community, and conversation. At The Garden Church, the line between the formal practice of breaking bread and other parts of the worship experience is not distinct. As we continue this chapter, we will unpack their versions of the shared meal and discover what's unique, different, and deeply familiar about the way people at these churches break bread together.

Feed and Be Fed: Feeding the Spiritual along with the Physical

Rev. Anna Woofenden, founding pastor of The Garden Church, sees food as a central connection point for the human experience. She is interested in how food connects with spirituality, in relationship to communion. Anna is also interested in how food is a basic human need that holds spiritual significance. Therefore, a large part of The Garden Church's practice centers around exploring how to feed people spiritually through worship and communion, and how to feed people physically without creating a stark demarcation between the spiritual and physical. Anna says, "We talk about blurring the lines at the Garden Church. We blur the lines between worship and working together and eating together."

Growing produce and sharing a meal at the The Garden Church is perhaps a representation of Genesis 1 and 2 in exquisite focus. Wasn't it on the sixth day that God said, "I now give to you all the plants on the earth that yield seeds and all the trees whose fruit produces its seeds within it. These will be your food" (Gen 1:29)? And then again in Genesis 2:8-9, "The LORD God planted a garden in Eden in the east and put there the human he had formed. In the fertile land, the Lord God grew every beautiful tree with edible fruit, and also he grew the tree of life in the middle of the garden and the tree of the knowledge of good and evil." Eve and Adam, as we know, end up being escorted out of the garden. Perhaps The Garden Church is a kind of reclamation project—if not a return to Eden, then a humble effort to participate with God in God's original vision of the relationship between human beings and the earth.

Rooted in the Christian tradition and Swedenborgian theology, the community holds the value that God's love is made visible as people are fed in body, mind, and spirit.

The Garden Church gathers on a lot between two buildings. Previously, the property housed a variety of temporary initiatives—parking, occasional event space, and a Christmas tree lot. Two beautiful brick walls border either side of the plot of land. One of the walls has a garden-themed mural on it, which was commissioned for a one-time party prior to the church taking possession of the property. You can see the green leaves rising against a blue background. The Garden Church leaders saw that mural as a harbinger of what they intended for the space.

It's a long narrow lot, and all The Garden Church activities take place in the outdoors on this lot. Worship space occupies the front third of the parcel. Tables occupy the middle section. The back third is dense with raised garden beds. Yes, the Garden Church raises food in the same lot in which it worships. The intense growing third of the lot once contained a mix of packed dirt and concrete. It was declared by others as "not grow worthy." Anna and her cohorts have changed that evaluation. Now, that section of the property yields over one hundred pounds of produce a month. The Garden Church is an urban farm *and* a place of worship.

The Garden Church's Sunday gathering, what most might think of as church in the traditional Sunday morning timeframe, takes place on Sunday afternoons. If you arrive a little after 3:00 p.m. you will be invited to work, contributing to the care of the gardens. This might include weeding, watering, preparing beds, planting, and harvesting.

Next, you and others in the community gather to hear a message, pray, and celebrate communion. Communion signals the transition of the worship service into their community meal. As Anna describes it, "We move from our sacred meal to our shared community meal, sing a blessing song, eat, and then have a closing ritual and song." At some point close to 5:30 p.m. you will hear Anna say, "Part of making church together is cleaning up together."

This is how Sunday goes at The Garden Church.

You can be part of any or all of the Sunday gathering because, according to Anna, "There's not one specific thing that's church. During Sunday afternoons at The Garden Church, it's all church. How do you want to participate?" In this way, the different parts of the Sunday gathering have continuity but are also permeable so people can come in and out as they are comfortable. This is reflected in the way that Sunday attendance is tracked. The attendance sheet reflects columns for "Work," "Worship," and "Eat" where congregants write down which part they are choosing for the day.

The Garden Church's motto is "Feed and be fed." It reflects the idea that everyone has something to offer and that everyone hungers for something, but it's not just physical food for which people are hungering. At The Garden Church the practice of breaking bread is expansive. Your body, mind, and spirit are attended to through soil, plants, and food.

Some people encounter The Garden Church on a physical level by receiving fresh produce. Some come solely for the community meal. Anna reflects, "We have a growing number of unhoused neighbors who come for the community meal, but then they start coming a little earlier for worship or the work hour. One of our unhoused attendees was directed to us as a church that might be able to provide him with food." During his first visit he explained that he didn't need food. What he needed was prayer. He ate at the community meal, but what he really needed was the prayer that happened at the end.

Anna says, "It's been really beautiful to see that when our Sunday activities are mixed up a little bit, we find out that we all have a deep need for both the spiritual and the physical nourishment. Meeting the physical need through food opens the door to a spiritual experience."

The Garden Church is not a feeding program; that is, it is not like a congregation that sets aside the first Monday of the month to offer canned goods from their food pantry. The Garden Church provides a spiritual experience in which food is the God-given resource. What is the correct language for all this? The Sunday meal is like a church potluck, but it is more than that. It's like a picnic because everyone sits down together at outdoor tables. But the designation of picnic doesn't capture its essence. It's family dinner. But it is more than a family dinner because those gathered aren't biological family. Indeed, on so many Sundays it is a diverse group; the line between people who come from their homes and those who are unhoused is pleasingly blurred.

How do people in the neighborhood who don't participate in the church experience The Garden Church? They do so with a little bit of confusion, a little bit of curiosity, and with gratitude too.

The Garden Church presents first and foremost as a community garden.

"I think that's how people first experience it," Anna says. "And then they see 'The Garden Church' sign and they ask where the church is."

Passersby and newcomers looking for a church find it curious and confusing that the answer to their question of, "Where's the church?" is "You're standing in it." Once the initial surprise is over (*this can't be a church, can it?*), people respond very positively. Local folks express appreciation that something beautiful is happening in this space. While some people have no interest in being part of a spiritual community, they are grateful that The Garden Church exists as a positive force in the community.

And it is a positive force. You can experience this if you choose. Anna is preaching now. The text is the transfiguration of Jesus as remembered in Matthew 17:1-9. Listen along. She's saying,

Let me set the scene a little more. For those of you who haven't been there, The Garden Church is not your typical church. We took an empty lot in the heart of San Pedro and transformed it into an active urban farm and outdoor sanctuary. We worship outdoors in the middle of the garden, with the ground beneath our feet and the birds and wind and sun above. And we work and worship and eat together right in the heart of our community. People are always walking by, all kinds of people, and we get to know our neighbors as we work and worship and eat together.[1]

Keep listening, don't let your mind wander. Actually, somehow it is easier to pay attention to a sermon preached outside than inside. Why is that?

I'm sure you all have your stories. Stories about how you saw a person, or a group of people in one way, until something changed and shimmered, and your assumptions and ideas of that person or group changed.

Maybe it was when you had that long, real conversation with a relative who has a different political stance than you. Maybe it was sitting across the table from one of our unhoused neighbors and hearing their story. Maybe it was the time you met a Muslim for the first time and encountered them as a fellow-human being, rather than an unknown group. Maybe it was when you hear someone's faith story, or learned you grew up in the same town, maybe it was through a photograph, or a piece of art. Maybe it was the quiet knowing that your heart needed to soften, to change, to be open to the many ways that the image of God shines and transforms humanity all around us.[2]

God shines and people become light in front of your eyes. The sun shines and plants produce food for you to share with others. This is The Garden Church. We believe it is a divergent church because breaking bread isn't regulated to an occasional activity among many. Eating together doesn't mean an occasional potluck. Many congregations have gardens, even community gardens. But few congregations have gardens that are as carefully connected to the theology and practice of the congregation's mission and vision as The Garden Church's is. To press the point, we have yet to find a congregation in which the garden is in the sanctuary (or the sanctuary is in the garden). The Swedenborgians say that "all religion is of life." This includes the food we grow and eat and share. Adam and Eve may have had to leave their garden. This faith community in San Pedro is finding its way back.

While The Garden Church's version of breaking bread includes actually working in the garden as part of the communal gathering, Simple Church puts its own spin on the practice of breaking bread. Let's move on to meet Rev. Zach Kerzee and the good people of the divergent church community he serves.

Farm to Table: Sustaining Church through Bread

The Rev. Zach Kerzee, founding pastor of Simple Church in Grafton, Massachusetts, is with a group of clergy. We the authors are present. Imagine you are too. Someone has just asked Zach to describe the essence of Simple Church. Zach says,

> I call us the farm-to-table dinner church. Our practice is eating with one another, sharing community meals, and talking about the ways that eating with one another across difference builds community and family relationships across spiritual divides. We've also taken on bread baking as a trade, which has helped us engage with the community and financially support ourselves.

If this is the essence of Simple Church, here are the elements to the backstory. Harvard Divinity School: that's where Zach was educated. Because of his experience at Harvard, he is used to being with others representing diverse religious realities: atheist, agnostic, Buddhist, Christian, Hindu, Jewish, and more. Simple Church rose, in part, from resources provided by the now-closed North Grafton United Methodist Church. Like many other divergent churches, Simple Church has no building it calls its own. It meets in another church's fellowship hall on the Grafton Common on Thursday nights. Like many divergent churches, this community of faith meets at a time other than Sunday morning, because some participants also attend congregations that assemble on Sunday morning.

There's still more to the backstory than Harvard, the United Methodists, and Thursday evening. There is the farm-to-table value; Zach works twice a week at Potter Hill Farm. The lead farmer of Potter Hill is a generous person. Zach is allowed to harvest enough food each week to serve at the Thursday evening dinner. This means the food you eat at Simple Church is grown within walking distance of where you have gathered for worship. One more important element: Simple Church runs a subscription bread service. The congregation rents kitchen space from another church and makes and bakes their own bread. Flour. Water. Salt. Yeast. "Our bread is simple," says Zach, "just like our church."

The practice of bread baking developed from the congregation's worship experience. Attendees observed that because communion is a big part of the worship service, it would be fitting to have homemade communion bread. Church leaders agreed and someone volunteered to bake the first loaf of homemade communion bread for the following Thursday. Zach began telling everyone that fresh bread for communion would be served that week. And then the bread-baking volunteer experienced a family emergency and had to leave town. The volunteer could no longer bake the bread that week. Zach recalls, "So I sat down at the computer and searched 'How to make bread.'" He found a basic recipe and baked his first loaf of bread. "I was a total novice. It's embarrassing to remember my poor kneading technique and how much sugar and yeast were in that first loaf. But that loaf was the best bread I had ever tasted!"

A local man, an artisanal bread baker, was regularly participating in Simple Church. The gentleman is Jewish and identifies as an atheist. He became curious about Simple Church and went once to try it out. At that time the bread baker told Zach that he was only going to attend once. He ended up attending for two years. He stopped attending because he relocated for a job. The gentleman's presence wasn't about a religious debate or what religious way was the best. His presence signified the mutual respect that Simple Church seeks to make real. It also represents the mutuality that is resourced when people break bread together.

And the bread baker's presence made Simple Church's bread even more pleasing. Zach now had a teacher who taught him the essential elements of bread baking.

"Zach, you do not need all that sugar and yeast in the bread. The only necessary ingredients in bread are flour, water, and salt. Mix in only a small amount of yeast and little to no sugar at all."

Simple Church participants persisted with their newfound enjoyment of bread baking. Week after week the bread kept getting better, more rustic, and earthier. Soon Zach saw the community as an extension of the bread baking. Making bread requires the coming together of the flour, water, and salt to make something completely new. Those few ingredients transform into a loaf of bread. So it is with the varied and different people who gather around Simple Church's table.

As Zach says, "When combined they make something better than they could be individually."

The loaves of bread and the new church were on parallel processes of growth and coming into being. But Simple Church's loaves were about to take on yet another facet.

People took notice of the bread and suggested that the church sell it. At first, Zach was reluctant to pursue this idea. But upon further reflection, and a thorough calculation of financial factors, he ascertained that a source of income beyond the giving of their regular thirty to forty attenders and some denominational support was imperative.

So Simple Church looked to the tradition of monastic communities who took on trades as a means of self-support. Monks brew beer, make cheese, raise crops, and sell their goods for income. Zach saw the possibility for Simple Church to sell bread for income and by doing so become more visible in the community.

They started selling bread at farmers' markets. Now revenue from bread sales is the church's number one means of self-support. During the farmers' market season, Simple Church bakes one hundred loaves of bread per week. During the rest of the year, they bake forty loaves per week. That's a lot of bread for a small church to bake. "All our bread is handmade. We don't use any machines," Zach notes.

Simple Church may not use bread machines, but they do have a head baker on staff who is versed in the science of bread making. The head baker is one of the reasons that Simple Church has other ways to expand their life of breaking bread. Also on staff is another pastor who will serve Simple Church as she starts a second location. Her funding model is going to be a catering service that hires formerly incarcerated people. This new breaking bread church will gather at a time and day other than Sunday morning too.

There are other innovations. For example, Simple Church also created a job-training program through the Grafton Job Corps. The church employs at-risk youth as apprentices and teaches them old-world bread-baking skills.

Bread baking and bread breaking isn't just a program of Simple Church, or an activity. It is a way of life that reinforces the deepest values of the faith community. Yeast. Flour. Salt. Water. They come together to make something new, a crusty-on-the-outside, pillowy-on-the-inside loaf of bread. So it is that Zach and others of Simple Church gather for worship—break a huge loaf of bread at communion—and they become the community of Christ.

We're back in the room where Zach is speaking with other clergy. He's talking about how long it takes to learn to make good bread. If you learn from a good teacher (as Zach did from his bread-baking friend) you can learn the essentials in about an hour. After that, though, you are learning each time you make a loaf. So, in some ways it takes a lifetime to become a bread artisan.

Such elemental ingredients come together to create such essential matter.

As Zach says, "There's nothing more different or simple than flour and water or water and salt, but when you put them together and they are just melding, it all makes something better than they could be on the individual parts."

This is simple. This is church. This is divergent.

Putting a New Spin on Breaking Bread

Simple Church "breaks bread" in multiple ways, which is a hallmark of divergent churches. This means that a practice commonly found in most churches is brought to life with a twist or an addition. The breaking of bread isn't limited to the altar, or the communion table, or kept in the confines of certain ritual actions or prayers. At Simple Church the practice of breaking bread includes work at a nearby farm, baking bread, selling the bread, and eating together as part of worship. At The Garden Church, breaking bread includes weeding the garden for the food that will feed people in need and everyone who gathers for Sunday worship.

Breaking bread together might seem so rudimentary, so natural, that no lesson and no reflection is needed. However, the dynamics of growing food, eating together, creating the conditions for both spiritual and physical nourishment are wonderfully complex. The dynamics are part of a practice with standards of excellence that, when achieved, support a range of religious claims and commitments.

When you eat a meal with another person, you are sharing an *experience* with another person. When you share a positive experience with others you're going to feel close to those with whom you share the undertaking. We are wired for connections through experience. For example, going on a trip with others bonds people together. Working on a project builds positive, emotional associations. People feel close to those they went to school with because they encountered a variety of school events together. The same dynamic is at work when people break bread together. It is an experience that binds.

Researcher Ayelet Fishbach says,

> I think that food really connects people. Food is about bringing something into the body. And to eat the same food suggests that we are both willing to bring the same thing into our bodies. People just feel closer to people who are eating the same food as they are. And then trust, cooperation—these are just consequences of feeling close to someone.[3]

Fishbach notes that sharing food together builds trust and cooperation. The dynamic may be largely unconscious, but it is real. It makes sense that faith communities that are meant to be places where people explore ultimate concerns and engage multifaceted possibilities about important matters like the nature of God, forgiveness, inclusion, service to others, death, and purpose would gravitate toward activities that build trust.

Divergent churches are hardwired for creating trust. The factors that make up the practice of breaking bread naturally develop among creative faith communities because the presence of food creates the opportunity space for virtues like trust and cooperation.

Remember chapter 5 on the practice of conversation. Many divergent church leaders use dinnertime as the time and place to talk about important matters like salvation, confession, the nature of Jesus, and much more. The presence of food lowers defenses and self-consciousness. The experience of a community working together to provide a meal contributes to a church culture that values honesty, listening, and vulnerability in conversation.

There are many creative congregations that make use of dinner church experience. The divergent churches we learned from do more than host dinners. The practice of breaking bread includes the real presence of seed, soil, water, grain, produce, homemade meals, and large loaves of bread—all together creating the conditions for deep consideration of Jesus and the claims and commitments he represents.

A significant claim and commitment that Jesus represents is engagement in the community beyond the church itself. It is to the practice of community engagement that we now turn.

Divergent Reflections

1. What are the ways in which your congregation breaks bread together? What are some of the primary rituals of such gatherings?

2. The Garden Church has a garden. What activities in your congregation get you closest to the soil?

3. Simple Church bakes bread. It is a valued item, and there are people in the church gifted at baking. What are the valued food items in your congregation? Are there items that one person (maybe more) is gifted at growing or making? How might your congregation make greater use of this food item to represent your religious claims and commitments?

4. How might your faith community practice breaking bread in a divergent way? Brainstorm creative ways to bring people together around food.

Chapter 8
THE PRACTICE OF COMMUNITY ENGAGEMENT

D ivergent churches reflect their context. They are the opposite of a franchise. That is, they are so rooted in their context it would be difficult to replicate a divergent church from one location to another. Divergent churches take on the characteristics of their surroundings. Recall how the Cowboy Church is set at a trail ride camp. Remember how the Community Church of Lake Forest & Lake Bluff assembles on a beach. In Floyd County, Virginia, Edwin Lacy leads the Wild Goose Christian Community that is steeped in Appalachian arts, including music, crafts, and dancing. These alternative faith communities and others like them put on the characteristics of the people, places, and pursuits around them. Mutual, reinforcing interests emerge between a divergent church and its environment. Divergent churches are not fortressed communities separate from their setting. In some divergent churches it is hard to tell where the world inside the congregation and the world beyond the congregation begins and ends. Even if you are deeply embedded in a divergent church—in its worship, education, relationships—it is as if you are still standing at the threshold of the church with a panoramic view of the world beyond. The people who worship God in divergent churches don't do so to retreat from creation. They find a spiritual home in order to be deeply connected to the world around them.

The connection to the world exhibited by divergent churches represents the practice of community engagement. This practice involves engaging those beyond the church for, with, and sometimes against others for the sake of embodying the religious claims and commitments of the faith community.

Of course, all kinds of churches practice community engagement. A church doesn't have to be divergent to host a food pantry, partner with a public school, or advocate for medical services for children who live in poverty. However, divergent churches take to social engagement in ways that are nimble, improvised, highly relational, and closely connected to the context in which they worship. Community engagement in divergent churches occurs at the intersection of the churches' often well-defined religious values and the needs and gifts of the local community.

In this chapter, we share stories of three divergent congregations and their social engagement. The characteristics named above—nimbleness, improvisation, relational connections, and attention to local context—will be evident. One congregation practices social engagement mostly *for* others. Another seeks engagement *with* others. A third congregation practices social engagement *over and against* existing social structures.

Community Engagement through Charity

"The beach church" is what Tom Dickelman sometimes calls the Community Church of Lake Forest & Lake Bluff (Community Church in short). Remember that this congregation has no members (though it has 275 active families). The congregation owns no building. The congregation has no debt. It basically has no committees besides a small finance group for purposes of order and integrity. The Community Church has no outreach or social engagement categories in its budget. Yet some years the congregation has raised more money for outreach than it has for itself. For example, the congregation started a charity in Africa and participants have raised more than $1.5 million and sent seventy-five people to the African community for short-term mission trips.

Community Church's various forms of social engagement are primarily expressions of charity. Some criticize charity. Some even say charity is toxic.[1] Yet, charity has a long history as a human practice. It is an integral part of community and social engagement. In 1 Corinthians 13, Paul equates charity with love for another. Charity is giving money to another person. Charity is feeding another person. Charity is helping a community rebuild after an earthquake. Charity is helping an urban, underfinanced high school basketball team have the resources to rise above its circumstances. Charity is sharing some aspect of your life *for* the benefit of another.

Being Nimble

For Community Church social engagement is not only charitable but also nimble. It is often improvised. The charitable work of the Community Church is not part of a strategic plan, or based on extensive external or internal assessments. Does the church track community demographics through social analytics? Does it discern through a planning process where its gifts and the world's deep needs intersect? No. Social engagement is agile. Leaders pivot with ease, like a power forward on the Chicago Bulls.

Such a pivot is the church's Adventures in Spirit initiative. Thirty people from the Community Church were going to Nepal on a spiritual adventure. Know that Nepal is a country where practitioners of Hinduism, Buddhism, and Islam live peacefully together, a place where adherents of different religions are positively influenced by each other (a Buddhist may incorporate elements of Hinduism into his or her practice). The Adventures in Spirit trip was consistent with what Tom says about the church's theological worldview: "We follow the way of Jesus, but respect and honor other traditions."

A week before the group was to leave, a devastating earthquake struck Katmandu. During that week the church designed a logo for this developing cause and created T-shirts that hung like prayer flags from trees in a Lake Bluff park where they were hosting a free concert just seven days after the earthquake. Even though it was a free concert, the congregation raised $35,000 through free-will donations.

How did this happen? As Tom says, "If we had a bureaucracy or committees, there's no way in the world this would have happened. I've lived in the community nearly thirty years and know how this kind of stuff works here. We don't have to convene an international outreach committee for every little detail. We can turn on a dime when the need appears." The Community Church has a nimble organizational structure. In this case, such a structure allowed decisions to be made promptly. The result was authentic charity in the form of $35,000.

Experiential, Collaborative Charity

The Community Church is also committed to experiential outreach. It creatively leverages resources to support other ministries and charities.

This is true for their Net Game project. This project supports the Orr Academy High School basketball team. Other sponsors besides the Community Church include the Institute for Nonviolence Chicago, the *Chicago Sun-Times*, and New Vision Athletics.

Orr Academy is located in one of Chicago's toughest neighborhoods. For the young men on the basketball team, the life challenge is this: "Stay out of jail. Avoid violence. . . . Remain alive."[2]

Along with the other partners, the church brings together the youth of Lake Forest High School and the youth of the Orr Academy for a pre-game meal, basketball game and barbeque. The event provides a high-profile model of how differing communities can join together. With the event donations, the Orr Academy High School basketball program receives needed support for the team to do more than simply remain alive. It provides for an already remarkable basketball program to thrive.

Some church partnerships lose energy because they become organizationally too complicated. Too many decisions have to pass through committees, teams, and councils, and the reason for the partnership disappears in the layers of bureaucracy. The Orr Academy effort is designed to encourage sponsor support while keeping the focus on providing a positive experience for the youth.

Engagement with Whimsy

Here is another example of community engagement and the Community Church. The congregation hosts a Dancing Bohemian Ukulele Team. Tom was at a wedding a few years ago and the groom played a beautiful song for his wife on the ukulele. Tom was inspired by the performance. So, Tom learned to play the ukulele. After that he and a few friends started a ukulele band (an accordion seemed too hard to learn). The nine-member band plays various gigs around town. About four times a year the band leads worship music at Community Church.

The story doesn't stop there; it doesn't stop at the boundary of a personal interest of the pastor or an occasional appearance in worship. Many people, in the church and beyond, were so excited about ukulele music that the church started the Bohemian Dancing School of Uke. People come to the church office to learn to play the ukulele.

As Tom says, "What happens with innovation is that if you pay attention, it opens the door for even more innovation."

In this case, creativity opened the door to more creativity (and fun) both within and beyond the congregation. What started with Tom's personal experience is now a community experience. In this way, the Community Church is salt and light for its adherents and neighbors.

There is a whimsy to the social engagement of the Community Church of Lake Forest & Lake Bluff. Social engagement for this congregation is often playful. Humor exists just below the surface of many of their community activities (*let's start a ukulele club!*). The tone is light, even fanciful. Tom has written, "We are serious about faith yet don't take ourselves too seriously."[3]

What makes divergent church ministry different from other faith communities? After all, many congregations provide charity. The special gifts of the Community Church of Lake Forest & Lake Bluff include the ability to improvise, to provide resources with little bureaucratic hindrances, and to add a playful element to its community contribution (a bohemian ukulele group!).

In your faith community, how would you approach charity if you had fewer institutional restraints? What would you do differently if you were empowered to be more playful? In what ways would you use improvisation to the advantage of those you seek to serve? These questions come alive for us in response to watching divergent churches provide charitable services for their communities.

Creating Mutual Relationships through Community Engagement

Now, let's turn to another form of community engagement. What does a ministry *with* others look like in a divergent church?

A group of clergy are talking about social services their congregations provide. One pastor says that the congregation she serves provides free mental health counseling (with licensed therapists) to people without insurance. Another clergy person describes a restorative justice program his congregation has been hosting for three years. "There's a lot of tears, hard work, and laughter going on," he says. A lay leader of a new church development says that they are partnering with a public school regarding character education.

The conversation turns to results and impact. How do you know if your work is making a difference? A leader of a divergent church, a house church network, says that their primary social engagement involves partnering with existing services regarding job placement. A person in the room asks, "How many people were you able to help find jobs last year?" The divergent church leader responds, "We keep track of that but that isn't how we measure success. We measure effectiveness by how many friends we've made."[4]

How does Gospel writer John remember Jesus's words? "I don't call you servants any longer, because servants don't know what their master is doing. Instead, I call you friends" (John 15:15a).

In addition to whimsy, nimbleness, and improvisation, divergent churches value relationships when it comes to community engagement. Divergent churches create community engagements that forge friendships. Though there are divergent churches that do ministry for others, the majority of alternative faith communities we learned from seek to engage *with* others, creating friendships that are mutual, relationships in which power differentials are minimized. This is reflected in the language used. Leaders of the divergent churches we talked to were careful to not categorize people either by stereotype or by social reality. The mentally ill are described as neighbors, not categorized by their diagnosis. The homeless are identified as colleagues, not by their social situation.

Divergent churches are effective at social engagement because they realign assumptions concerning who is learning from whom. Those who are in need are recognized as wise. Those who are without necessities are welcomed as partners. Such partners become leaders with the divergent church in solving difficult problems.

Community Engagement as an Ultimate Concern

So, now we are ready to reintroduce you to Jonathan Grace, the pastor of Church at the Square, a United Methodist worshiping community that is anchored with Highland Park United Methodist Church in Dallas. We met Jonathan first in chapter 5 as we learned about the practice of conversation.

Approximately seventy to eighty people worship on Sunday at Church at the Square. The gathering space is across from the Cottages, a housing complex designed to support residents who have been identified as chronically homeless. Subsequently, many of the worshipers are formerly homeless. The church developed from CitySquare ministries (a comprehensive social service agency led by Larry James whom you will meet later in this chapter), Highland Park United Methodist Church, and the United Methodist local judicatory.

Church at the Square's ultimate concern is both worshiping God and being a change agent in a broken world. Recall that a common theme among divergent churches is that they attend to God *and* another ultimate concern (what we call "church plus"). This is true for Church at the Square.

Ultimate concern: What matters most to the congregation?

Church plus: The way in which a congregation attends to that which matters most.

The ultimate concern for Church at the Square is care *with* the homeless and those otherwise economically marginalized. Compared to more established churches, it is difficult (and often unnecessary) to differentiate Church at the Square's vocation as a worshiping community from its work with the homeless and the mentally ill. Is it a church? Is it a homeless ministry? Is it an organization that advocates for justice? Church polity was not written with Church at the Square in mind.

Friendship and mutuality are conceptual sacraments for this alternative faith community. Jonathan and his new friends are shaping social engagement activities that are consistent with these values, and yet are represented by unique, highly contextual experiences. Nothing is the same twice when one is doing ministry with friends as opposed to doing ministry in response to a social science statistic. The positive deviance is wondrous. That is, the solutions to intractable problems deviate from some best practice written in a "how to" manual. Instead, the solutions are found within the community itself (and its relationship with Christ). The solutions deviate positively from accepted norms.[5]

The Power of Here and Now Revelation

One thing we've learned about divergent churches is not to underestimate the strange, rare, yet powerful disclosures of the Divine. God speaks. Tom Dickelman of the Community Church received a revelation on the steps of the chapel (chapter 4). For Jonathan, his epiphany came during a morning jog. This is the story of how Jonathan experienced God calling him to community engagement *with* others.

Jonathan was serving as pastor of a monastic community called the Bonhoeffer House in East Dallas. The Bonhoeffer House located itself next door to Refugee Services of North Texas. Bonhoeffer House dedicated its ministry to refugees. Unfortunately, at almost the same time that Jonathan and his community moved in, Refugee Services moved out (to a better building). What to do next? The Bonhoeffer group had no idea.

One morning about 5:00, Jonathan is jogging. He is praying to the Holy Spirit. "Come on God," he prays. As he is praying, he runs by CitySquare (the social service agency). He didn't know what it was at that time. He passes by the I-30 overpass. He's still praying. He looks over. He sees a homeless encampment. He sees thirteen homeless neighbors curled up with backpacks and blankets (such encampments are not always visible because homeless neighbors are always being told to "move on").

At that moment, Jonathan says, "God moves me, spiritually moves me, something I'm not used to."

Jonathan says, "God literally widens my gaze to see something in my world that was already there."

It doesn't take long before Jonathan begins doing homeless outreach. He says that he and his colleagues were awful at it. "We just didn't know what we were doing, handing out terrible ham sandwiches and such."

At one encounter, a blanket goes from Jonathan to a new friend we will call Eli. Eli is part of the homeless encampment. A conversation begins.

A few days later, Eli drops by for soda. Soon Eli is praying with Jonathan and others at the Bonhoeffer House. A friendship begins.

Jonathan is interested in learning from Eli about how to be most helpful.

Eli offers constructive criticism. "Okay, here's what you are doing wrong. Here's what you are doing right, sort of. Here's what you should be doing."

Ministry *with* begins.

It's conversation that evokes change in Jonathan's method. But it is more than that too. A mutual style of ministry that includes friendship is rooted in Jonathan's desire to hear a homeless person's feedback and apply the newly discovered wisdom to the program. Of course, Jonathan still has power in his relationship with those he serves; the way he's using that power is what makes the program *with* rather than *for*.

Given the desire for mutual ministry, let's illustrate how meaning-making and community engagement intersect at Church at the Square in a way that shares the responsibility for interpretation and testimony. It's Sunday. You walk to the worship site. It is outdoors. You can see the Cottages at Hickory Crossing—homes for the formerly homeless modeled after communities created in the Gulf States after Hurricane Katrina. As Jonathan is greeting people before worship, there are others preparing the lunch that will be served right after the service (the practice of breaking bread).

A woman walks up to Jonathan, tears flowing down her cheeks.

She asks Jonathan, "Is Jesus God?"

Jonathan is thinking this is one of those theological questions that was settled long ago. But he also wonders, why should I assume that it is settled for everyone?

She continues, "Is Jesus God? Because I'm confused. The Bible says he is, but he's also praying to God. What is it and if I don't get it right am I going to hell?"

Jonathan responds, "Well, short answer, yes, Jesus is God, and no, you're not going to hell if you get it wrong."

But Jonathan is already thinking of next week's sermon. He's going to preach on the Trinitarian controversy and that our knowledge does not save us; God saves us.

During worship Jonathan hands the microphone to a woman. She stands straight and tall and speaks, "Just three months ago I was living next to some of you in that tent city. Now I have a home. Now I have dishes. Now I have food in the refrigerator. Now I'm learning to cook."

The distance between the Trinitarian controversy and finding one's way out of a tent city is not so far apart at Church at the Square. The distance is bridged by friendship, desire for mutuality, and revelations from God that make community engagement inescapably linked with the Divine.

The value of mutual relationships in ministry with others is evident in deep ways at Church at the Square in Dallas, Texas. Though the church itself is new, the work from which it developed has been ongoing for many years. To understand how a culture of ministry "with" becomes rooted in a divergent church, we want to take you back to what we will call *the before the before* of this alternative faith community.

The Genesis of Mutual Ministry

The virtues that make up Church at the Square's practice of community engagement did not come from a textbook. The virtues developed several years ago when the nonprofit—CitySquare—was beginning to take shape in the mind of Larry James.

Remember that Church at the Square exists as a worshiping community in relationship with Highland Park United Methodist Church, CitySquare, and the United Methodist denomination. To understand Church at the Square's mutual practice of community engagement, we want to introduce you to the early community work of Larry James, the current leader of the robust nonprofit CitySquare. By doing so, we can show how the innovative practices of this divergent church are an example of how the tried and true has become brand-new.

Engagement with (rather than for) others goes back to an experience Larry James had in the 1990s. Larry was asked to work with a congregation that provided various services to people who lived at the margins of society. He says, "I didn't say yes because I had the training or qualifications." For Larry, "It was the Gospel thing to do."

Along with volunteers, Larry met with people struggling with life issues and attempted to come up with ways to help. On the very first day a volunteer approached Larry, who was standing over a large coffee pot.

The volunteer asked, "What are you doing?"

Larry said, "Well, I'm making coffee. I like coffee. I bet you like coffee. I know that our guests are going to be coming and they will probably like coffee. Maybe we can get to know each other and figure out what to do."

The volunteer responded, "Don't you know that if you make coffee, these people will never leave?"

This encounter represented the opposite of mutuality. This was not Gospel. It may have been church work, but it was not Gospel. It was then that Larry knew he was going to have to "fire" some of the volunteers.

One day, though, as Larry tells the story, the good Lord finally took pity on him. Larry is meeting with three Latina mothers and their children. The three women are strangers to one another. Larry doesn't speak Spanish. The women are working together speaking what English they know to overcome Larry's lack of fluency in Spanish. As a group, they aren't making much progress.

That is until Josephine Ortiz walks by. Josephine had already been interviewed. At this moment she is coming out of the grocery store part of the building back through the interview room. Larry stops her.

"Ma'am, could you please help?"

Josephine was surprised (more like startled?). Here was Larry asking for help. That's not how the equation worked in this place. She is there for help, not Larry. But Larry needs her help and he knows she is bilingual.

"What do you need?" she asks.

Larry answers, "I need someone to translate."

"Certainly," says Josephine.

Josephine puts down her groceries. She gently directs Larry to attend to the children. Josephine proceeds to conduct the interview (remember that she had just been interviewed by Larry). It doesn't take long now. "What are your names? Where do you live? Tell me about your children. What are your needs?" The three women need support with the rent, utilities, and groceries. This can happen. This does happen. As the women leave together, now friends, Josephine turns to Larry and says, "Larry, I could come back tomorrow and help you."

Josephine Ortiz came back tomorrow every day for nine years.

And the practice of ministry *with* friends began.

This way of being with those in need, the way of mutuality and seeing the gifts of those being served, was sealed in a revelation that Larry James had later the same day he met his new friend Josephine Ortiz. We want Larry to speak for himself:

> I went upstairs into my office. In that old building there was a plate glass wall. I could see out into the community. There were people everywhere. There was a bus stop. There was a telephone booth. There was a crack house. There was a crack campground. People were trying to get away from the drugs. People were trying to go toward the drugs. People were buying and selling. People were on the phone. People were trying to get on the bus. Most people were just trying to watch their backs. And I had an experience that I still from this day don't completely under-stand, but I heard a clear word from God and I was not trained nor was I brought up to hear a clear word from God. And God said to me, "Son, you are a dummy." And I said, "Indeed." And God said, "I don't have time to give you the entire list of why this is true, but I'll just give you a couple of examples." And I said, "Yes, Lord." God said, "You don't have any idea what this community needs. You can't possibly know." Check, got it. "Furthermore, when you conceptualize the idea of need, it's always in terms of finances and monetary solutions. And that is no way to look at or to regard anything for which I am responsible," God said. So, I immediately think of Josephine and I look back at the street and I see all these people and I realize that the social capital, the neighborhood intelligence, the experiential seniority, the embed-ded nature of my friends whose names I do not yet know; this is what we need in order to change everything. It's not going to be volunteers coming from outside with bad attitudes. It's going to be by engaging Josephine and her friends.

This revelation is the genesis of a divergent church, the Church at the Square, that wouldn't begin until some twenty years later. It is an example of how divergent churches build on the practices of those who have come before but adapt the prac-tices in creative ways to their contemporary context.

Creating a New Social Order

Let's go back one more time to Church at the Square, actually to a revelation that helped Jonathan hold a vision for the church before it began.

Jonathan is out in a neighborhood one evening. He and others are interviewing members of the community. Jonathan already knows many of the homeless folks he is encountering because he met them at the nearby tent city. After two hours of interviewing, he ends up in the parking lot of a 7-Eleven. Jonathan sees a homeless friend of his. His friend had enough money to purchase a large pizza from the convenience store. The friend walks out the door carrying the pizza.

"Hey Jonathan."

Jonathan says, "Hi there, how's it going?"

They start talking. The friend offers Jonathan a slice of pizza. Now, Jonathan has already eaten. He's feeling full. He's thinking, *I'm not feeling that great, and at this moment I don't really want any gas station pizza, and anyway I've been shaking hands all night so my hands are filthy.* Jonathan is thinking, *There is every reason in the world why I don't need this gift right now.* (Oh yes, the power differential, there is always the power differential present in these friendships.)

So the friend offers again, "Here, have pizza with me."

"No, thank you, I've already eaten."

"Come on, take a slice."

"No, that's all right," says Jonathan.

"Take a slice."

In that moment Jonathan changes his mind and takes a slice of pizza and eats. He sits down with his friend and they share a meal, a blessed meal. Jonathan has another divergent moment of revelation: *My friend is serving me communion, yes, that's what he is doing.*

Jonathan has passed the ordination exams. He knows that in the United Methodist Church there is clarity about what constitutes communion. Yet in this moment the orthodoxy is breaking apart through the power of the Holy Spirit. The friend is black. Jonathan is white. The friend is poor. Jonathan is middle-class. These differences are disappearing in the presence of encountering Christ through 7-Eleven pizza and the holy reality of friendship. This is the practice of community engagement. The tables have been turned on the social order, at least for a moment. The reality of Jesus's edict to become friends is, right here and right now, both in and beyond time. It feels brand-new.

What else is brand-new? At the very least (or the very most), the practice of community engagement at the Church at the Square seeks to be a safe place where, in this place at this time, the power of society's unjust structures has been minimalized. Such power has been minimalized through the message of Jesus's desire for friendship, and the establishment of a divergent community of Jesus that meets needs—emotional, relational, and physical—*with* one another.

Which brings us back to friendship. How does God intend our society to be? How does God intend for us to interact with one another? That's the challenge of community engagement for Church at the Square. If you were a leader at Church at the Square, your ministry would be to demonstrate to your new friends, the homeless and the formerly homeless, that they belong, that they are loved. *This is a place where you are welcome to linger. You are not going to be told to move on. You are wanted here.*

Taking Social Action through Community Engagement

Sometimes community engagement in divergent churches involves charity, doing something for someone. Sometimes community engagement in divergent churches involves mutual relationships, doing good with someone else. At Valley and Mountain in Seattle, Washington, community engagement is linked to social action. This social action includes doing good with others and, sometimes, it necessitates action *against* a principality or power.

Valley and Mountain is a United Methodist church, though like most divergent churches that are linked with a denomination, the affiliation isn't the primary marker for the congregation. For Valley and Mountain, its ultimate concern beyond worship for God is its involvement in the community. The lead pastor, or convener, is John Helmiere. In addition to being pastor at Valley and Mountain, John is the co-founding director of the Hillman City Collaboratory, a social change incubator in Seattle. It is through the Collaboratory that Valley and Mountain engages its broader community.

The Collaboratory shares its building with the church. Inside the Collaboratory are some twenty-five or more social movements, nonprofits, or simply (or not so simply) people with dreams. John describes the Collaboratory as a mix of activists, artists, homeless folk, and assorted others seeking social justice.

The Mixing Chamber: Real Life Collides with Dreams

If you want a neat and tidy place to do your social dreaming, the Collaboratory isn't your place. Relational connections often take place in the mixing chamber, a two-thousand-square-foot room that's open to the public. Take a look inside and you will see people eating a free meal. You'll see two people talking in a corner over coffee. In another part of the room art supplies are dispersed on a table and a young man appears to be drawing. Some people are sitting on a couch; others are talking on phones. Some of the people in the room are homeless; some are not. Some are seeking to change housing policies. All of this contributes to a cacophony of sound and untidiness not unlike that of a well lived-in community space in a college dormitory.

At times in the mixing chamber real life collides with dreaming like the sound of an out-of-tune chord on a guitar. You could be sitting in the chamber having just received a mystical revelation that might lead to change in an oppressive city law and your epiphany is interrupted by a shouting match because two emotionally hurting people just knocked into each other.

"Hey!"

"You are in my space!"

On Sunday the mixing chamber becomes the worship space. The morning service features gospel and world music. The sacrament of communion is served at every gathering. The afternoon service is less conventional. It has three movements. First, a mix of music and content for reflection. The second movement begins when people break into Encounter Groups. You can choose to experience a variety of spiritual practices: singing, yoga, silence, consideration of a social justice issue, and more. The third movement is a meal: simple in substance, vibrant with conversation.

If you are at either celebration you sing. Watch the song leader reach for the guitar. The chords sound. You know a little about folk music. The song sounds familiar. Ah, yes, it is "Satan, We're Going to Tear Your Kingdom Down." You start to sing. Wait. The lyrics have been changed (John says, "We change the lyrics to lots of our songs"). Yet you catch on soon enough:

> Tyrants, we're going to tear your kingdom down
> Tyrants, we're going to tear your kingdom down
> You've been building your kingdom, all over this land.
> Tyrants, we're going to tear your kingdom down.

The congregation sings the other verses. After tyrants it becomes Caesars.

> Caesars, we're going to tear your kingdom down.

After Caesars it becomes Deceivers.

> Deceivers, we're going to tear your kingdom down.

John Helmeire and Valley and Mountain relate to an activist God. John and others at Valley and Mountain experience God as integrated into the fabric of the universe—all around us, listening deeply to us, empathetically engaged. If God is like this, the church should be like this too. This is the theology that informs the Collaboratory. This is the theology that forms Encounter Groups on Sunday afternoon. And it is this theological worldview that leads Valley and Mountain to social activism.

Taking a Stand Against

It is Holy Week. Many of us know Holy Week begins with Palm Sunday. Then the Maundy Thursday service recalls Jesus breaking bread with the disciples in the upper room before his arrest. Good Friday memorializes the death of Jesus, crucified by the powers that be on a stony hillside. Holy Saturday, in some traditions, is the time for holding vigil. All these activities lead to Easter Sunday, the Lord's Day that celebrates God raising Jesus Christ from the dead; the power of death and evil has been vanquished.

During Valley and Mountain's first Holy Week as a congregation, about twenty-five people participate in worship. John asks, "What should we do, this being our first Holy Week?" John reads the Gospels, particularly what is known as the passion narratives—the events leading up to and including Jesus's death. John discerns that it's Monday when Jesus goes to the temple and flips over the tables of the money-changers. This is a bigger deal than generally acknowledged. Flipping the tables is probably a significant factor in Jesus getting arrested and killed. (Try interrupting the floor of the New York Stock Exchange and see how long it takes for you to be moved on, probably not so gently.) John observes that the other parts of the passion narrative (as told in the Synoptic Gospels) don't happen without the crisis in the temple. Yet, many folks don't talk about this.

John talks with others in the church about Jesus and table turning. Others agree with him—yes, this is important. They want to learn more. They learn that the temple wasn't just a religious institution. It was the economic center for Jerusalem. As told in Matthew, Mark, and Luke, it was Passover. For Jerusalem Passover was the height of economic transactions. After all there were many visitors in town. The modern equivalent might be Black Friday at the mall, Cyber Monday on the Internet, or the summer season at Disney World. It was at this moment that Jesus chose to disrupt commerce on the busiest week of the year at the central economic location in his part of the world. He is going to anger the economic elites (which means he is going to anger the political and religious elites too because they are all feasting together).

John Helmiere has a revelation (remember that revelations are a key element to discerning social engagement in divergent churches). *Let's not do a service. Let's go to the temple and flip some tables.* The leaders look around the neighborhood (they are committed to *this* neighborhood, the heart of Hillman City in Seattle). Over there is a branch of a national bank. As John says, "At that time, the bank was messing people over right and left." So the congregation goes to the branch. They raise a ruckus. They distribute leaflets with information about where the credit unions are located. The group walks inside the lobby. Someone makes a speech (they thought about literally turning over tables, but didn't).

Table Turning Monday is now an annual activity. More and more people at Valley and Mountain participate; some at the Collaboratory are involved. In 2016, a Valley and Mountain intern sat down with representatives from a Collaboratory partner called Standing Against Foreclosures and Evictions (SAFE). This group hosts foreclosure blockades. If there's an unjust foreclosure in the works, SAFE gets to know the person who comes to them for assistance and they organize people to block the house from those seeking to enforce foreclosure.

The intern and the activists at SAFE connect with a woman experiencing foreclosure. She has started to worship with Valley and Mountain, leads small groups, and has met new friends at the church and at the Collaboratory. It is this woman who is going to lead Table Turning Monday this particular year.

The day arrives. If you are there you will later tell your friends how you walked behind the woman as she pulled a red Radio Flyer wagon through downtown Seattle. Inside the wagon is a model of her house, covered in chains. You will recall the first stop is City Hall. Speeches are made. Folks aren't shy talking about Jesus, but there is some restraint when it comes to Jesus talk because not everyone here is religious. Then the woman "closes" City Hall. She puts up a big sign: *I foreclose on City Hall.*

The pilgrimage continues until it arrives at another national bank branch. Perhaps if this is your first Table Turning Monday you might feel a little nervous by now (do folks ever get arrested doing this?). The officials at the bank try to stop the crowd. But you and the woman with the red wagon and the others get in before the gates are closed. The officials are on their phones. They are threatening to call the police. They are not used to their lobby being noisy and untidy. Valley and Mountain put up the foreclosure signs. The officials pause on their phones long enough to tell the security person to take the signs down. He says with a wink, "I don't think I'm authorized to do that."

John says,

> This all is discipleship. It is to have our people get a little bit scared, get a little uncomfortable because this is where we need God, this untamable, unnamable power to change and to hold and to heal us. We can only get there if we begin to surrender some of our safety and our security and our comfort and our ego, and that happens when you are doing something you're not supposed to be doing, because of the right reasons. This is discipleship.

What are the marks of community engagement in your congregation? Does your congregation practice social good for, with, or against others? What would it be like to challenge the powers that be knowing that you, knowing that we all participate to varying degrees in supporting unjust systems? What conditions and factors would need to be present for your congregation to not only provide charity for others, serve with the homeless and economically challenged, but also stand against some aspect of the social structure?

Conclusion

The practice of community engagement is highly visible in divergent churches. In almost all divergent churches there is some element of charity, caring for others by doing something for another. In many divergent churches there is a driving desire to be friends with those who are served. A divergent community doesn't do ministry *for* the homeless; the community *is* the homeless. *The word "with" signals where God is present in the space between people who are sharing a common experience.* Some divergent churches take up social action as part of the practice of community engagement. Such action represents a stance against unjust social structures.

Consideration of community engagement naturally leads to consideration of hospitality. What is it like for a congregation to welcome those who are somehow different than the majority culture in the local community or in the church itself? We've already observed in our chapter on shaping community that the vision to welcome everyone is both beautiful and problematic. Yet, hospitality still exists as an essential practice of divergent churches. After all, divergent churches exist to be a spiritual home for spiritual refugees. This does not happen without concentration on the practice of hospitality. In the next chapter, we explore this practice in more detail.

Divergent Reflections

1. Would you describe your congregation's community engagement as more charity, mutual work together, or taking a stand against an issue or institution?

2. Let's consider two practices together. Does your congregation's community engagement involve the practice of breaking bread together? If so, tell a story about such an experience. If not, what might be one group you'd like to break bread with? What might be a first step?

3. What is one of the most innovative community engagement experiences in which your congregation has participated? What were the marks of innovation present in the activity?

4. What community needs are most evident in your location? How would you test if your answer is accurate? Would your congregation address this need more like the Community Church of Lake Forest & Lake Bluff, or more like Church at the Square, or Valley and Mountain?

Chapter 9
THE PRACTICE OF HOSPITALITY

Hospitality is hard work. Hospitality sounds like a practice about loving people and approaching strangers with unconditional regard, which is true in some circumstances. It has a happy ring to it. However, a more robust, realistic view of hospitality includes discernment about attachment (how close can I get to those I don't yet know?) and boundaries (how do I not lose myself in relationship with someone very different from me?). The practice of hospitality involves balancing safety and challenge in the midst of relating to an untamable God.

What does hospitality look like in your congregation? Perhaps hospitality is linked to welcoming visitors in worship. You may serve on a team that delivers a loaf of bread to the homes of those who have visited worship. Or maybe hospitality is related to turning your fellowship hall into a homeless shelter four times a year. After all you are familiar with Romans 12:13: "Contribute to the needs of God's people, and welcome strangers into your home."

Imagine you and others prepare a meal for the homeless of your town (usually pasta and salad) and you have learned the names of several of the guests. You drive home that evening feeling like you have indeed welcomed strangers into the house of God. You have contributed to the needs of God's people. At this moment, the practice of hospitality has a warmness to it.

Or maybe, on another occasion, you have experienced discomfort hosting strangers. As you buy groceries for (let's call them) Sam and Diane—as part of the deacons' ministry—you invite them to worship. They come the following Sunday. And after worship two women report their purses missing. You aren't certain that Sam and Diane are the culprits. But it sure feels that way. So there you are, experiencing

105

the tension that comes with hospitality. How do you confirm trust? When should you draw boundaries?

In the world of business and entertainment, some companies are outstanding practitioners of a form of hospitality—customer service. You are at Disney World. You have lost a fast pass (the tickets that let you bypass the long lines). So you go to the station where you can receive assistance. You are ready to make your case—the kids are tired, you left the hotel room in a hurry, your spouse doesn't do well in long lines. The attendant looks at you with a smile and says, "Let me see what I can do for you." She's back in two minutes with the passes you lost and three more. This is, we suppose, a kind of hospitality. Yet, as nice as it is to be treated this well, the transaction is not so much hospitality as it is excellent customer service.

In the divergent churches we studied, hospitality is more than customer service. *For divergent churches, hospitality involves the pursuit of the Divine at the same time as welcoming both neighbors and strangers, while coming to terms with the differences between people.*

It is good and right and beautiful to become friends with those different from you or who are otherwise strangers. In divergent churches, hospitality is a spiritual activity that enhances your experience of God and contributes to the possibility that God will be experienced in the space between two or more people. Hospitality, in divergent churches, isn't a way to recruit more members. Hospitality is made up of various activities that bring people closer to God and to one another. In this way, divergent churches integrate the practice of hospitality with their pursuit of meaning-making.

How Does Difference Function in a Divergent Church?

This chapter will explore the practice of hospitality in divergent churches. One way to explore hospitality is to observe how a congregation welcomes those different from the majority either in the congregation or in a particular cultural setting.

How does one measure difference? In the early church, difference in the Christian community was observed as whether one was Jewish or Greek, a slave or free person, a man or a woman (Gal 3:28).

Some differences are less obvious than others. There are nuanced differences such as whether one learns visually or orally, whether introverted or extroverted (is it possible for a church to have a personality in this way?). More often differences are calculated by overt sociological differences. Some congregations are multiracial. Most are not. Some congregations are assemblies of people with widely different economic conditions. Most are not. Some congregations are homes to people with widely different political views; the socialist passes bread to the neo-conservative at communion. Most do not contain people with such a diverse range of political views evenly represented.

In Indianapolis, after a "religious freedom" law was long debated, many business owners posted signs in their storefronts that stated, "We welcome everyone." Are there limits to welcoming everyone? As Anne Williamson of WAYfinding, one of the divergent community leaders we interviewed, observed, "We believe deeply in openness, but we're not an organization without boundaries. If someone came in and said, 'My belief system says to kill people,' we would say, 'You are not welcome here.'"

Again, divergent church leaders are keenly aware of the tension between trust and boundaries.

In the divergent churches we studied, the practice of hospitality relates to other practices such as shaping community, conversation, and community engagement (chapters 4, 5, and 8). For example, at Church at the Square in Dallas, the members of Highland Park United Methodist Church who are more economically prosperous find themselves in crucial conversations with people who are homeless or formerly homeless. Such conversations involve both welcoming strangers and coming to terms with difference. At Galileo, as we learned in chapter 4, the challenge of welcoming a particular person led the community on an authentic examination of conscience related to its values and its behavior. For the Community Church of Lake Forest & Lake Bluff, social engagement supported an annual basketball game between high schools that, in terms of demographics, have very little in common (chapter 8). How people talk with one another, how the faith community is organized, the way the church relates to the wider community all inform and form the practice of hospitality in divergent churches.

The juxtaposition of hospitality and meaning-making has led the divergent congregations we learned from to live in the tension of being a safe place and being a place of challenge regarding difference and welcoming the stranger. We talked with divergent churches that have become gifted at providing a safe place for spiritual refugees. Alternatively, we talked with divergent leaders challenged by hospitality. How far can you go in testing the expansiveness of belonging for the sake of pursuing the aims of God?

So, let's look more closely at divergent churches that are practicing hospitality in pursuit of the Divine. Sometimes the goal of hospitality is creating a safe circle for those who otherwise don't feel welcome in more established churches. Sometimes, the goal is being challenged by differences. Let's first examine the former of these goals.

Hospitality and Providing Safe Space

Rev. Monique Crain Spells leads Levi's Table in Indianapolis, Indiana. Levi's Table is a new church project of the Disciples of Christ denomination. Its focus is on young adult African Americans who seek to follow Jesus in an open and affirming community.

Monique also serves Christian Theological Seminary in Indianapolis. Students sit in her office. They talk with her about what it is like to find a church home. She hears similar themes to their stories. Many of the African American students are experiencing religious dissonance. They go to worship, hear the sermon, and think, *That's not congruent; that doesn't make sense.* When the students search for a worshiping community that makes intellectual sense, they feel disoriented. The students have been formed by the vibrant worship of their home churches. They know worship as a celebration. Worship contains rhythmic preaching. The songs are soulful and heartfelt. Yet, in the worship settings where they feel most at home, the theology that is preached doesn't link with what they are learning about social justice, particularly in terms of affirming LGBTQ persons. A student will comment to Monique, "I know I can feel safe in an open and affirming church, but I'm not going to experience worship that excites me, or preaching that speaks to my experience as a black person. Where do I belong?"

This kind of disorientation led to the creation of Levi's Table. It is one of the divergent churches we studied that is hard to pin down in a category: is it a church, a study group, or a spiritual community? The Disciples denomination calls it an "emerging church fellowship." To us, it is a divergent church. It is a safe place for African Americans who are open and affirming to the LGBTQ community and who want to honor the rich strengths of more established black churches.

The name "Levi's Table" is intentional. It comes from Luke 5:27-32. Jesus invites Levi, a tax collector, to follow him. Levi leaves everything behind and goes with Jesus. At home, Levi hosts a large dinner party for Jesus. Those in attendance include tax collectors and other unnamed guests. Monique says she has studied and studied this passage. She is on a search to figure out who the "others" are. Monique says, "No matter how much I have studied, I cannot find a clear definition as to who these others are." Monique notes that when people are not named in scripture, it is often because they are considered "lesser" people. Monique says, "The people are either women or outcasts or the sick or perhaps a prostitute, a leper, the poor, or whomever."

Levi's table as represented in Luke 5 is a place for spiritual refugees.

What happens at this contemporary Levi's Table? The group gathers for study, worship, and communion. The time for study begins with people giving updates on their lives ("this has not been an easy week for me"). They pray together. Then the group engages the scripture for the week. If you are there, you will read a portion of the Bible passage. Everyone does. If there aren't enough verses for everybody, the group will reread the text until everybody has spoken. After hearing the passage, you will sit in silence with the group. Then Monique will share what is on her heart in relationship to the text. Others follow with their thoughts. Maybe you will have something to share too. Then more silence, followed by the sacrament of communion.

Creating a Safe Space through Study, Communion, and Cultural Engagement

The people of Levi's Table also participate in cultural engagement. These are occasional experiences, sometimes three times a year, where the faith community experiences an art exhibit, reads a book, or views a movie. Then they interpret the cultural experience in terms of scripture, faith, and their life experience.

For example, the community engaged Toni Morrison's *Beloved* together, the Pulitzer Prize–winning novel that tells the story of the resilient freed slave Sethe.

Early in the book there is a short dialogue that captures the intractable challenges Sethe faces. The conversation is about the death of Sethe's mother-in-law.

"Was it hard? I hope she didn't die hard."

Sethe shook her head. "Soft as cream. Being alive was the hard part."[1]

Yes, being alive is still the hard part for African Americans for whom the Civil War story of *Beloved* remains too present.

Beloved begins with an epigraph from Romans 9:25: "I will call them my people, which were not my people; and her beloved, which was not beloved" (KJV). The passage provides abundant material for a faith community that experiences being displaced, the opposite of belonging.

In addition to cultural encounters with art and literature, Levi's Table participants have attended "don't sleep" meetings, gatherings related to the Black Lives Matter movement (a national movement with local chapters that affirms the validity of black lives). These gatherings carry the slogan *stay woke*, encouraging not only conversation and proclamation against systemic racism, but also encouragement and strategic thinking about action. They say, "Let's do something." Those in the Levi's Table community have also participated in training and meetings with Dr. William Barber (the Protestant minister and political leader).

The goal for all these activities—study, communion, and cultural engagement—is the creation of a safe space for African Americans to explore elements of progressive Christianity while maintaining connection with the positive power of African American worship: praise that is participatory, celebrative, and artistically wise with abundant rhythm and rhyme.

The practice of hospitality at Levi's Table provides a secure place for people of faith who otherwise feel like they are in exile from other Christian communities.

Levi's Table provides an intellectual safe place, as well as an emotional and physical safe community, for exploration of the authority of scripture, the exploration of LGBTQ issues, and strategic contemplation of other social realities like violence against blacks.

Monique says, "I wanted a space where people felt free to ask questions, free to grapple with texts, free to doubt if they wanted to. But more importantly, free to speak who they were, where they were. It is still a homogenous space as far as African Americans' participation. This is so because safety is such a crucial piece."

Staying True to Hospitality While Diversifying

Sometimes hospitality welcomes strangers whose presence diversifies a community. One of us might be a leader in a predominately upper-middle-class Caucasian church and in walks a Latino family on Sunday morning. We jump to action. "We're so glad you are here." Someone fetches coffee for the adults and lemonade for the children. A person in worship notices that the parents aren't following the liturgy because it is so new to them. So this person moves and sits with the family to help them through the liturgy. At the end of service, the pastor introduces herself and arranges for a home visit on Thursday evening.

Or maybe you are sitting in worship and notice behind you that someone is speaking over the preacher. The voice sounds angry. He isn't making sense. You can feel other worshipers getting anxious, tightening up (yes, you can feel this in a group). You wonder if this person is mentally ill, perhaps psychotic. You think, *Someone ought to do something.* Then you remember times when you haven't been all that together, not psychotic—no—but maybe depressed or anxious. You just knew how to hide it better. You breathe deep. Your heart softens.

Or if you are Caucasian, you have walked your white self into a Dr. Martin Luther King Jr. Day service. The first thing you notice is that the music is not what you experience in the contemporary service at your suburban nondenominational church. The percussionist and the Hammond B-3 organist are leading with a skillful, displaced backbeat. You feel out of place. And then you think, *This is disorienting.*

Even if you aren't a stranger you can feel strange at any number of worship gatherings.

Levi's Table is a place where African Americans can trade the experience of feeling strange for the experience of feeling safe. The practice of hospitality takes on the values of intellectual integrity and validation related to different sexual orientations. It's an affirming space. Hospitality begins with creating a safe space for a small group of people wanting to contest the boundaries of their previous religious experiences and the boundaries of a majority white, heterosexual culture.

Until recently, to maintain the community as a safe space, Levi's Table has been, not a closed community, but one that was not promoted as a public gathering. Just like many new churches, Levi's Table needed to first build a core group. The first participants—clergy, former clergy, seminary students, those who sought out Monique for counsel—found out about the group through relationship networks or networks within the Disciples of Christ denomination.

Recently, Levi's Table has gone public and attracted new people. The presence of new people has created the need for strategic thinking related to hospitality. In any group, one can get used to the safety that is already present. Then, new people with new opinions and counter thoughts appear. Compared to group norms or compared to the goal of safe space, the new opinions and new thoughts can sound less refined, less thoughtful (*wow, I wish he hadn't said that*).

The challenge for Levi's Table is to practice hospitality with the new person (the previously unnamed person, not unlike the anonymous persons who gathered at Levi the tax collector's house in Luke 5). Those who are already participating at Levi's Table seek to model behaviors that make Levi's Table a safe place. The challenge is to impart the church's practice of protected place to new participants.

It's okay to be silent at first.

Make sure your thoughts are what you want them to be before you say them.

Practice empathy.

Consider how your observations might affect another.

The new people need to experience safety. Yet, those who are already part of Levi's Table still need a safe place while welcoming those who may not yet fully know the conditions of spiritual shelter.

The divergent church experience of providing a safe place for those who otherwise haven't found a spiritual home isn't just a hospitality issue for Levi's Table. We heard this theme from almost every divergent church leader with whom we spoke.

Providing Spiritual Shelter

Remember the Cowboy Church mentioned earlier in chapter 3? The Cowboy Church, led by Doug Hanner, a Nazarene minister, represents a different theological worldview than Levi's Table. Yet, the two faith communities share the importance of providing spiritual shelter for those who otherwise don't feel comfortable in church.

The Cowboy Church worships on Sunday at Midwest Trail Ride of Norman, Indiana. The gathering place is adjacent to the Hoosier National Forest. The church participants have more than two hundred acres of riding territory available to them. Before or after worship on any given weekend, worshipers take to the trails, such as Birdseye Trail. On top of a quarter horse, you will ride past a lake, a creek, old homesteads, and even a cemetery (the dates have been worn by the weather). There are hitching rails along the way so that you can stop, dismount, and look around at green trees and pillowy clouds in the sky.

When Doug thinks about Cowboy Church he pictures men and women, boys and girls (faces he knows), who live their weekdays in rural settings. They have no connection with a Christian community. Or, they have been part of a faith community but feel burned or disenfranchised or disappointed in some way. They've sworn off the traditional church.

Doug says, "The church I serve is made of people who say that if they ever would go to 'real church,' the ceiling would fall in."

In Doug's tradition, the Cowboy Church is considered a Church Type Mission (CTM). It has progressed through a series of transitions, from church plant to an affiliated congregation and now CTM. Doug is hesitant, not unwilling, but hesitant to move to the next step of being a full-fledged denominational congregation. The reason he is hesitant is that he worries that some of his flock might get excluded. "My people make great Christians," he says, "but not so good Nazarenes." They smoke. They drink. They cuss. Not more or less than, say, other Christian populations like contemporary Presbyterians or Disciples. But in the holiness tradition of the Nazarenes, such behaviors are discouraged, if not considered taboo. So, when Doug sets up for worship on Sunday and places the Folgers coffee can out on the table as the offering plate, he is aware that Cowboy Church represents a safe place for those who would be invited to a party hosted by Jesus himself but likely excluded from other "religious" gatherings.

Divergent churches are sanctuary churches in the sense that the gathering space is meant to be a place of spiritual refuge or safety. It is shelter from religious storms. Hospitality is, in one sense, directed inward, providing immunity from the particular cultural or religious barriers the participants have experienced. The practice of hospitality in divergent churches creates a consecrated place for those estranged from majority experiences of religions. Such churches are expanding the meaning of hospitality in terms of welcoming the stranger. The majority of the adherents are strange to or estranged from the prevailing communities of faith. Therefore, the new divergent communities are providing a hospitable alternative.

As much as creating a safe place is essential to the practice of hospitality, particularly when supporting the faith of those who have had negative experiences elsewhere, more is needed. At least that is what we also learned from divergent churches. For faith development, there is a need for adherents to summon courage and engage with those who are different. Hospitality involves safety, yes, but it also involves introducing just enough challenge into experiences so that you befriend those who are different from yourself. We now turn to the challenge of hospitality as divergent churches seek to include a greater variety of people.

Hospitality and Challenge

The film *Little Man Tate* is about an intellectually gifted seven-year-old who struggles mightily in social situations. The movie begins with his seventh birthday. No guests show. It's not easy being different.

As the story develops, Fred Tate's mom makes difficult decisions trying to balance Fred's emotional and educational needs. Fred's mom is determined that his intelligence not keep him further separated from emotional connections. She succeeds. At the end of the movie, there is another birthday party, Fred's eighth birthday. This year the room is full of friends, young people, and adults representing various economic, social, and cognitive groups. Fred's voiceover narration says, "I once got a fortune cookie that said, 'Only when all who surround you are different will you truly belong.'"[2]

Let's make our way back to WAYfinding. Welcoming different perspectives is essential to WAYfinding's purpose. From the beginning, WAYfinding has been diverse theologically. It is diverse in terms of LGBTQ representation. It is diverse in terms of age and participation of females and males. However, it is not diverse racially. Anne Williamson, the leader of WAYfinding, decided it was time to change this. So, Anne said to her group, "Let's decenter ourselves. Let's allow the voices of those who are not having voice in our community right now take center stage."

This led to an experience called *Black Lives Matter and White Privilege.* Many have gathered at the Design Bank, an innovative design firm owned by an African American woman. Those in the room the night of the event notice that it is full to capacity. Hosting the WAYfinding event at a female, black-owned business in an area of town with limited financial resources and gang violence is part of Anne's decentering strategy. The photographer is an African American. The panel discussion leaders are all paid so the event wasn't just the white community saying "come educate us for free." Anne looks around the room, and more people of color are present than white people.

What would it feel like if our voice wasn't given the most space?

The evening is good but not entirely comfortable. Anne stands at the front of the room. She is looking at index cards on which people have written questions. Some of them make her feel uneasy. Yet in the uneasiness, something is happening.

One participant, a white man, says, "This changes my life; this is changing the trajectory of my life."

Another white male, a member of WAYfinding's advisory team, says, "The way this material is presented makes me never want to get involved with this cause."

Can a church create a culture where discomfort is part of the accepted experience? A mark of a divergent church is its willingness to chase after discomfort rather than run from it. For Anne and WAYfinding, faith is a willingness to listen deeply to others (and the other inside you) and align your life to that which you hear. It's not about a particular set of beliefs. It is about a way of being in the world. This way is a hospitable way. It involves creating space for questions *and* challenge, particularly the possibility of being challenged by those who have a different perspective. This is how assumptions are tested. This is what moves us to listen ever more deeply.

The Balance of Safety and Challenge in Hospitality

Hospitality in scripture involves both safety and challenge. Recall the Good Samaritan parable (Luke 10:25-37). A traveler has been robbed, beaten, and left for dead in a ditch. Three people come by. First a priest and then a temple helper pass by on the other side. A third man from Samaria comes traveling along, and he treats the victim's wounds with olive oil and wine. The Samaritan helps the injured man to an inn and pays for lodging. That's the safety part of hospitality in the parable. A secure place has been provided.

What about the challenge? The challenge develops when you consider who it is that the first-century listener would identify with in the story. Homiletician David Buttrick suggests that the first-century common person listening to the parable would not have identified with the priest or the temple helper. Buttrick also suggests that the first-century listener would have expected the third person (in terms of first-century rhetoric) to have been one of them, a regular peasant-class Israelite. The listener would have expected the third person coming along to be one of them and thus the hero in the story.

Instead, Jesus inserts a character of ill repute, the "bad" Samaritan. (That's the only kind of Samaritan there would have been for first-century Palestinian Jews.)[3]

So who is left for the story listeners to identify with? That's right, the person who has been injured. The person in need of help. This person is receiving help from one of the most culturally despised dwellers in his or her world. Jesus's message: your life might depend on accepting hospitality from a confirmed adversary.

Gospel stories like the Good Samaritan parable inform hospitality in many divergent churches. Hospitality in this parable is full of challenges. It means never rule out the possibility that the only one available to help you out of a dire circumstance may be the person who makes you feel the most uncomfortable.

Time after time, we heard stories of divergent churches willing to relinquish control. This letting go almost always involved risking relationships with people who were different—or "other"—than the majority of the congregation. The churches didn't offer a program (we are going to host the homeless four times a year), but rather a way of life (we are going to be friends with the homeless; some of us are the homeless).

Remember Rev. Anna Woofenden, the pastor of The Garden Church in San Pedro, California (we met Anna in chapter 7). Anna is preaching to the people of The Garden Church on Transfiguration Sunday. She is telling the story of an experience, something that previously happened during worship at The Garden Church.[4] This is a sermon within a sermon. Listen carefully.

Anna says that while scripture was being read she noticed a man hovering outside the gates. Anna waved at him. He didn't come in. The man walked a little further down the fence and looked through.

As Anna was passing the Bible to the next reader, she whispered to Connie (a Garden Church participant gifted at hospitality), "Would you go do your friendly, welcoming thing?"

Connie popped up and went over to the man. Isaiah 58:6-7a was being read:

Isn't this the fast I choose:
  releasing wicked restraints, untying the ropes of a yoke,
   setting free the mistreated,
   and breaking every yoke?
Isn't it sharing your bread with the hungry
   and bringing the homeless poor into your house?

Connie listened to the man. He was standing there in slippers; with his tousled hair he looked like a person who knew the street much better than a home. After talking for a while Connie went back inside the gate to gather a full plate of food for the gentleman. The man accepted the plate. Yet, he was not ready to come in through the gate. He said goodbye to Connie.

Anna continues the story:

When Connie came and sat down we were about to start the sermon, but rather than opening my prepared text, it seemed right to first acknowledge the sermon that had just happened in front of our eyes. Connie shared that the man had not eaten for two days and was so hungry. He knew that The Garden Church was a safe place and wanted to come in and knew he was welcome, but he "just wasn't ready quite yet."[5]

As Anna continues to preach on this Transfiguration Sunday, she observes that God is revealing God's shimmering self in many different ways. She says she is noticing more and more "these moments of transcendence; these moments where I can see beyond the everyday, or beyond my veil of prejudice and not knowing, and see in another person the face of the Divine."[6]

If you are present that Sunday you feel the shiver down your back as Anna ends her sermon, this sermon within a sermon. You see, the gentleman at the gate came back. No, there isn't a perfect ending to this hospitality story. The man didn't come through the gates and magically become a fully realized participant in the unfolding story of The Garden Church. No, you feel the end of the sermon inside your body because of its to-be-continued quality. Anna says,

> When our hungry neighbor came by the gates later that week, I waved from the back where I was deadheading basil. He paused by the front gate, in his shorts and old bed slippers. He still wasn't ready to come in. But as he paused, and waved, I saw a faint glimmer and glow in his face. God shining through.[7]

This is how a divergent church lives in the tension between trust and boundaries. This is how a divergent church begins to negotiate the open hospitality of Jesus with the sometimes hard reality of life. It happens at the threshold of garden gates and around dinner tables and even on horseback trails.

Conclusion

What has been your experience with the tension between safety and challenge in terms of making room for people in your faith community? A mark of the divergent churches we studied is that they are willing to live with the tension as an unsolvable problem. Divergent churches experience the need to create safety for the spiritually homeless. But that is not enough for a fulsome practice of hospitality. So, divergent churches also acknowledge their privilege and seek to find gracious ways to learn from those who live with different realities. But this too is not enough for a fulsome practice of hospitality. One more factor needs to be considered. The additional factor is the divine reality that God is the Other who ingeniously provides the stranger (and sometimes threatening one) as our helper, and whimsically invites us no-names to feast at the table. This hospitality business is not a smooth enterprise. If you want to be treated like a king or queen, go to Disney World. If you want to experience the daring landscape of God's realm, visit a divergent church.

Which is what we do in the next chapter. For some time, through this book, you have heard indirectly, through us the authors, about these divergent churches and their leaders. In the next chapter we want you to hear directly from them with as little facilitation from us as possible. We want to get out of your way and let you enter a conversation with the divergent church leaders of this book. You are invited to Levi's home. Come on in. Pull up a chair. The dialogue is about to begin. We hope you feel safe here. And challenged.

Divergent Reflections

1. In what ways have you experienced your place of worship as a safe place?

2. Has there been a time when you felt at odds with your faith community or another faith community because of who you are or what you believe?

3. What have you learned about hosting people who are not like you?

4. How might your church make hospitality a way of life rather than an activity or program?

Chapter 10
THE VOICES OF DIVERGENT CHURCH LEADERS

W e the authors entered this book project with questions and curiosity about the landscape of religious life in the United States. So far the book has been us as authors sharing what we've learned. Now we share directly the divergent church leaders themselves, focused on three pressing questions. As authors, we are "silent" in this chapter, hoping that you will benefit from hearing only the voices of divergent church leaders.

We posed the first question:

"WHY DO YOU STAY IN A RELIGIOUS SPACE AS OPPOSED TO CREATING A SECULAR ORGANIZATION?"

Edwin Lacy from Wild Good Christian Community:

For what I was trying to accomplish it wasn't an option to do otherwise. All I was trying to do was offer a place in which people who were not drawn to either traditional or contemporary worship, and consequently left Christian community, had a third alternative where they could be part of the Christian faith. My theory is that of the droves of people that have left the church in the last thirty or forty years, many have not left their self-identification as Christian. They just have no options for a Christian community that fits them. So I tried to create one that would be attractive but also very meaningful without being antitraditional or anti-contemporary worship style. I wanted it to have a worship style in a type of Christian community that would have meaning for them, and to give them what I suspected they desired but didn't know where to find. I can't do that in a secular place. It had to be a worshiping community.

Lisa Cole Smith from Convergence:

The lines between artist co-op and worshiping community are very blurry for us. We left it open so that there could be real conversation between the two worlds. This speaks to this question about why it's important to stay deeply rooted in a faith tradition. The challenge of how to do that has been a fundamental question for us. When we started, I had little knowledge of other odd forms of church going on.

So, there was skepticism about why we were creating Convergence as a church-related entity. Wouldn't it be easier to just be a parachurch or an arts organization? And there was skepticism about why we weren't spending more time "building a church" since that's what we were supposed to be doing. But, we started with the desire to form a community with culture creators of faith. And, I think for me, part of it was trying to create a place where people like me would truly feel at home being all in with our creative selves, and also be all in with our spiritual selves. A place to be fully who we were created to be. I wanted to host a place where the two spheres belong together. That's what we have to offer to people. That's part of the vacuum that I found: there aren't many places where it feels safe to be authentic spiritually seeking, especially if you are an artist, even in church. There is a need for that kind of space. We've intentionally made even our grounds and buildings an environment where people can inhabit and explore the intersection between arts and faith even when there isn't an official activity happening.

But then on the other side, it's been important to make it possible for people of faith to encounter these creative people because our hope is to feed back into the church to spawn innovation and rebirth.

We then asked our second question:

"DO YOU CONSIDER YOUR DIVERGENT 'CHURCH' TO BE A CONGREGATION?"

We posed this question over dinner and went around the table giving each person a chance to answer. Most answered with a straightforward yes. However, a few of the divergent church leaders gave lengthier answers to the question.

John Helmiere from Valley and Mountain:

> We are a drop-in center, a business incubator, a worshiping community. So just one slice of us is a congregation. But the Collaboratory (business incubator) is, I've realized, a congregation too. It's just a secular congregation, a non-faith specific congregation.

Others around the table asked John to elaborate. Here's what he said:

> We have this building, it's awesome. It's a mix of a drop-in center for the homeless, or just lonely, or busted, broke-down folks. So, during the day, it's this space. At night, it's a dancehall, art gallery, social change fund-raiser venue. And, there's a co-working element to it. And, on Sundays is the church. In direct response to the question "Are you a congregation?" the Collaboratory is not a Christian congregation. Regarding Valley and Mountain, even though I talk about Jesus and the Bible and we sing Christian songs every Sunday, when talking about Valley and Mountain I almost never say it is a Christian church. This is because that declaration makes everybody in the room have to identify as Christian. And, they have not consented to that. And so, actually, in our welcome talk we explain that one's spirituality or belief is not a litmus test for you to belong at Valley and Mountain. You're included and there's a place for you at this table no matter what, without condition. So, that's why we don't say Christian.

Anne Williamson from WAYfinding:

> I struggle with what congregation means. I love when WAYfinding has community events and two people who've been participating in different WAYfinding groups walk in, see each other and say, "You do WAYfinding?" and the two knew each other unrelated to WAYfinding. There is this connection; I don't know if it's congregational in the way that is being talked about. It's an open question.

121

Chapter 10

Lisa Cole Smith from Convergence:

Yes, however, the lines between artist co-op and worshiping community are very blurry. We have a small worshiping congregation, but then there's a large community of artists and community members who intermingle in a lot of different ways and in a very real, though nontraditional, sense they are our "congregation."

Tom Dickelman from The Community Church:

Yes, we are a congregation, but we don't have members. If membership is a mark of what constitutes a church, we don't have that marker. We've existed for almost nineteen years, but we've never had a member. People show up if it fits. And, if they really find value then they put something in the hat. But we don't have and have never had members. I still haven't heard a reason why we should have members, because for us, it doesn't seem to fit with what faith is, which is this dynamic, growing, evolving experience. So, how do you take one set of values, sign your name underneath it, and say, "Okay, here's where I am period"? So, we don't have members.

Katie Hays from Galileo:

Galileo Church doesn't have members, but we have co-conspirators in the Gospel. Co-conspirators are the people who have made a covenant together for one year at a time to prioritize the mission of Galileo Church. We stole the one-year covenant idea from Church of the Savior in Washington, DC. And, we do that every year on Pentecost. Every year everybody's covenant is dissolved and people decide again whether they can do it for another year. At that time, we also talk about some habits of life that demonstrate that we're prioritizing the mission of Galileo Church. The word *co-conspirator* indicates that we think we're on to something that not a lot of people get. And, that it's kind of risky, subversive, and therefore delicious. But being a co-conspirator or not doesn't change the way you interact with the church. There are lots of people who come to Galileo who aren't co-conspirators, so the little nut of co-conspiracy is much smaller than the wider community of people who interact with our church in all kinds of ways. Over four years, I have good examples of people moving in and out of the co-conspiracy given their own life circumstances. For example, they might say, "This year, I'm going to finish my dissertation. I really can't prioritize the mission of Galileo Church this year." That has so much integrity.

"DESCRIBE HOW YOU KNOW WHEN YOUR CONGREGATION IS FLOURISHING."

John Helmiere from Valley and Mountain:

> I sense flourishing when there is deep joy being inculcated in people when they participate. I think about folks, in my church, who have gone to their first protest. It's a scary thing for them. They're not confrontational people. They weren't raised to be that. Or they never thought that they had a voice or that anybody would care what they had to say. And, that's a weird kind of example to give for joy and flourishing, but I feel like there's a deep sense of joy in that when you realize that you have some power. And, that you were created to have some power.

Tom Dickelman from The Community Church:

> I'm kind of old-school in a way. I think people show up and if they put something in the hat, those are measures that have some value. But, those by themselves wouldn't be enough. I think the Spirit speaks to us through our gut feelings. And so, that to me is the most important kind of feedback—what's going on inside. That's how I interpret how we're trending and how we're doing.

Anne Williamson from WAYfinding:

> Authenticity is important to us, so as a leader, what I think is one of the greatest markers in terms of flourishing as an organization is when people start to talk about WAYfinding. I think that some people come to WAYfinding skeptical. They may even be secretive about it in their life. Their family or friends don't necessarily know that they're participating in a WAYfinding group. And so, when they start to talk about WAYfinding to others in their life, I know that there's something about who we say we are and who they're experiencing us to be that is in alignment. Because if that were not the case, they would not be willing to share about our community. That always feels like a significant marker.

Lisa Cole Smith from Convergence:

There's a moment at Convergence when the conversation goes from "you" to "we" and "us." And that's when I know there's a shift for that person. They've entered into the "Convergence experience" and are no longer standing on the outside looking in. And that is an indicator of flourishing because we are engaging God together and not staying in our individual spaces, removed and simply intellectually observing. I also think it's when people are willing to be honest and take off the mask of fear. They're afraid to be honest in a religious context because they're afraid it's going to get them kicked out. When they're willing to unmask in front of each other, it results in spiritual growth.

Katie Hays from Galileo Church:

We think about the integration of the human person at Galileo. We're all closeted in a lot of places, and especially at church. If my high hope is that my queer sister or brother can come out and be the same person everywhere all the time, that hope might start at church, if it's a safe place to be out. Many people at my church are only out at church. There have been people who come to Galileo and go in the bathroom and change clothes, into the clothes they really want to wear. They sit through worship and then they go to the bathroom and change back into their "regular" clothes to go home or back to their campus.

So, when they start to experience more and more integration of themselves, that's a good sign for them personally. But when the church is a place where lots of people are coming out and becoming less bifurcated, and with less of a sense of "This is a special safe zone," that is a sign for me that we are doing all right. But this is not just about LGBTQ people coming out. It's about everyone coming out. We have a joke we tell about going to traditional church on a Sunday morning. You get to the door and somebody's there to greet you, and they say, "Hi, how are y'all?" And the answer is "I'm fine, how are y'all?" And then, you go in the church and that's the last conversation you will have had because that's all anybody really wants to know.

And so, can church be a place for real selves? I know that Jesus really wanted people to be their real, beautiful selves in his presence. Picture the John 4 story of the woman at the well. Jesus wants for her to be able to say what's true about her life, and say it in the presence of Jesus without the shame associated with that.

Tim Kim from Root and Branch:

When I sense there's shared joy and the same spirit of joy in our conversations even when they are difficult. I think a shared experience is really important. I noticed this shared joy when I see moments of people being really vulnerable.

And, the other part—and this is a harder part that we haven't seen as much—but I think really defines Root and Branch as its best self, is being able to have conversations that are counterintuitive to our expectations of one another. So, in a conversation when we are, for example, espousing progressive political values but someone brings up that they are also pro-life, can that type of honesty come forth and people not lose their minds? A conversation like that is a sign of true community. Such conversations are signs of authentic relationship that are important to flourishing.

Zach Kerzee from Simple Church:

I spend more time thinking about this than any other thing when it comes to innovation. Because the two things that people don't want to talk about with vitality are numbers and money. Because with the numbers question, they say we don't care how many people are there; we care how deep we go with people who are there. I see this disconnect because like any other institution, any other business, if you don't have people that are coming and genuinely wanting what you're providing, it is seen as a failure. If you don't have people coming to get what you're providing, that's a really good indicator that you should be providing something different, right?

I don't know why the church hasn't been held to this standard. I joke about the two or three gathered thing, but it really has become like a crutch, I think. If nobody's showing up to your party, you have to throw a better party. I think that butts in seats is actually a pretty good indicator of if you're growing.

I also recognize that it's not the only indicator. But then, if a congregation's only means of self-support as a community is passing the plate then your sustainability is built on having a ton of people there. If your only way of raising money for your community is the number of people, and if you have any expenses, and churches cost money because we live in a capitalist society and you're relying on three or four people to bankroll your church, that's not good either.

So, if we're going to say that butts in seats are not our primary indicator of vitality then we have to supplement it with some different way of raising money as a community. For us that's trade, specifically selling bread at farmers markets. But, yeah, I think you can't have your cake and eat it too. Either numbers are your key source of vitality, or you have to find another way to pay for the church.

For a dinner party, ten people gathered is about the right size. But, if we walked into a church building with ten people in it, we'd call it a failure in any sized chapel. If we're trying to pay for full-time pastoral staff, rent, and everything else ten people isn't going to cut it.

Tom Dickelman from The Community Church:

This is why for me innovation has to have a "so what" to it. Innovation needs to be more than a creative idea; though clearly a creative idea is important. Innovation is a creative idea that is actionable and provides value. Innovative congregations that are going to be sustainable and flourish need to have some impact, some measurable outcome that people can experience.

"YOUR CONGREGATION REPRESENTS AN ALTERNATIVE FORM OF BEING CHURCH. DO YOU THINK THAT FAITH OR BELIEF IS BEING RECONSTITUTED TOO?"

John Helmiere from Valley and Mountain Church:

I don't think a consumer model of church is what's represented among us. Do I think that we represent a belief in a consumer model where one affirms a principal, an abstract notion or concept? No. I think belief is something that you embody, you commit your whole self to. So it's not just that you commit to faith with your brain, but you also commit to belief with your wallet, through your relationship to a location, with your time, your whole being.

Tom Dickelman from the Community Church:

I agree with that. Yes, I really agree with that. My sense is there is absolutely a reconstitution of faith. It's not so much about belief and that intellectual assent, but people nowadays I think, who at least come in to our church, they're not so much coming to church because they want to figure out how to get to heaven. They're not going to church to get forgiven for that really big sin so they can be okay with God. I think they are human beings trying to find their way, trying to find spiritual connection and a way to live their lives that feels authentic and real. And that's not about belief per se—belief is part of that, but a small part.

Katie Hays from Galileo Church:

Galileo is in the buckle of the Bible Belt. I go to a church full of people who've been really rejected from church because of who they are, or because someone in their family or their colleague or maybe their best friend or whatever, and they just really think God gave up on them. So, we have these big blocks up on the stage where we host worship. One set of blocks says, "God's love is real." Another set reads "God's love is for you." Then another set of blocks says "God's love is worth it." And that's a correction of something that our people were told for a really long time, which is that God's *judgment* is real, God's *judgment* is for you, and God's judgment is *not* worth it. So, we flip that whole thing around, learning to believe that God's love is the realest thing in the world and that it is for you, that's huge. So, yeah, we're reconstituting faith week after week.

Zach Kerzee from Simple Church:

This has been said so many times it's almost cliché. Martin Luther's aim was not to start a new church. He wanted to fix the problems he saw in the Catholic Church. It was out of love for the church universal. He said the things he said, made the reforms that he did, out of love for Christ and the community of Christ. So I think what we're doing is to get at the heart of what church is supposed to be, or at least how we feel church should be. It's not that we are reinventing the wheel. It's almost like we're trying to get the wheel back on the vehicle. We're tightening the lug nuts and getting ready for the road again.

Jonathan Grace from Church at the Square:

I'd say it's God breathing new life into spaces. I grew up in Wichita Falls, Texas—and I knew a lot of people who were so adamant about going to church on Sundays and then were jerks the rest of the week, and that infuriated me. So is church just a social club that meets for an hour? Or is your encounter with Christ really transforming your life? It's great to work in a place where you can see our neighborhood in Dallas, new homes being built and people moving in, and so there's a lot going on materially in our location. In this way faith is more than simply nodding your head at some doctrine. There is a physicality to it. We are also nurturing the spiritual, the emotional health for folks who have struggled horrifically under terrible circumstances. I'm thinking about the Valley and Mountain experience with turning over the tables on Monday of Holy Week. That's emotional stuff. Jesus is angry. It's righteous anger. It's okay that the people at Valley and Mountain are angry. How do you express the reality that Jesus is angry? So, faith encompasses the emotional life too.

Anne Williamson from WAYfinding:

There is a worldview that sees progress as linear. There is a worldview where that progress is aiming toward the truth. Or that a single truth exists, and we're trying to get to that truth. So it goes that if truth is singular then God is singular, that is, there is one correct reality of God. Maybe one can still hold that truth is singular, I'm not sure. This way of seeing the world, a singular truth, has a parallel with church. For some in the congregational world there is a right way to do church and a wrong way to do church. And if you have the right way, then you have success. If you have the wrong way, then you don't have this capitalistic version of success. I feel like what I'm seeing among divergent or alternative churches is that there are unique expressions of being church—some things are similar—but in the actual life of the congregation there are very unique and different expressions of God's Spirit. This is intentional. It's not about some of us getting it wrong and others of us getting it right. It's the Spirit moving through each of us in different ways based on our context, and our gifts, and our histories. It is in this way that it feels like a reconstitution of belief or faith.

Tim Kim from Root and Branch:

What I'm doing often feels like therapy for people who've had really bad religious experiences. So there is a way that they're being healed. Our work involves telling people you're actually okay and good as you are. But, I can't say right now where that will end up for them, because I don't think that's the end goal. It's not that you just get some affirmation and you're like, "Okay, my life is great now." We want to nudge or push people toward something else that's better, that's still beyond just them being like "I'm okay, and whether we get there or not or what that looks like, I can't really say. I only have an idea." I'm one of these people who thinks that human nature doesn't ever fundamentally change. What's in the Bible represents human nature for us today as well. If that's the case, then reconfiguring is something we always try to do but never quite get to. Faith and belief play the same parts within human nature today as they did a thousand years ago. So is the transformation we are trying to bring about today not a comprehensive shift but just a little nudge? That wouldn't be such a bad thing in my opinion. It might be the only thing we've got and also a much better way of thinking about this stuff. But ultimately, I don't know. The jury's still out on whether new forms of congregating represent a whole new way of relating to God. My guess is no and that's just the way it goes.

Edwin Lacy from Wild Goose Christian Community:

In the stories we tell about our faith communities, I hear over and over again themes related to hospitality, community, and relationships. I wonder if one thing that we may be reconstituting related to belief is about being connected. Jonathan at Church at the Square says that people with mental health issues that are part of the worshiping community often act out when a relationship connection has been broken. They are isolated. It seems to me like, at least in the twentieth century, church supported conformity around belief. Maybe one of the things that we are doing regarding reconstituting faith is valuing connection instead of conformity; connection to each other as Christians, connection to Jesus Christ, connection to where we live. We end up with very interesting people at Wild Goose. We have a retired professor who has done a lot of studies with sociopaths and especially mass murderers. He has interviewed and been on-site right after the first responders and what he is learning about these tragedies is that the accused or the perpetrator is isolated from others before the event. When the perpetrator has survived, and my friend has interviewed them, it all comes down to being disconnected. Those who commit violence all felt isolated and that was the commonality between all of their psychosis. This is a tragic way to talk about the need for community and relationships, but it does highlight that what we are doing is really important, because a spiritual connection is the deepest connection. And the spiritual connection is moving from conformity to connection.

Divergent Reflection

1. What activity does your church do beyond worship that makes it essential that your faith community is a church and not another kind of assembly or organization? What would be lost if this activity was not integrated into the faith community?

2. How do you know when your congregation is flourishing? In what ways are these marks of flourishing noted, affirmed, or celebrated?

3. In what ways has the faith your church expresses changed in the last several years? For example, do people talk differently about relationships? How do people talk about truth compared to a generation ago? How is the person of Jesus Christ represented in different ways?

Chapter 11
CONCLUSION

Through this book we have introduced you to creative, alternative congregations—what we call divergent churches. We have considered the nature of innovation. We have reflected on what constitutes a church. Having introduced you to these churches, we have invited you to consider their life together through the framework of practices—tried and true religious activities that take on new life in these divergent settings.

Now we want to consider with you what difference this information makes.

Our journey with these divergent churches has led us to a deep appreciation of these congregations. We hope you have experienced some appreciation for these congregations too. We believe they are a bright hope for the future of church life.

We admire their risk-taking. Almost all of the divergent churches we studied have modest resources. The leaders have taken personal financial risks. They have chosen the road less traveled.

We admire their creativity. The leaders of these churches have adapted universal human practices into unique expressions of faith. The Cowboy Church has turned a horseback trail meeting hall into a sanctuary. Convergence has joined with the punk rock community to make art. The Community Church of Lake Forest & Lake Bluff has made ukuleles an instrument for community engagement. At Church at the Square it is wonderfully difficult to tell where social services begins and ends and where worship begins and ends; the two are integrated in a holy and wholesome way.

We admire the way these divergent churches are bringing people into religious community who otherwise would not be in such a community. Levi's Table is a safe home for African Americans wanting to honor the best of their religious experience while welcoming progressive explorations concerning sexual orientation. Root and Branch Church in Chicago welcomes edgy theological conversation that allows participants an alternative to strict nihilism through exploration of belief in a way that deconstructs orthodox understandings of the Creator. Divergent churches are sturdy homes for religious refugees.

So, we hope that you can, in your own way, affirm the work of these congregations as we have come to validate their life together.

Lessons

Our hope is that affirmation of these congregations will lead you to consider what aspects of divergent churches you might consider for your setting. Please regard these stories as your permission to innovate. What lessons might you take from these divergent churches and apply to your setting?

Some of you are associated with established congregations. So the topic for contemplation would be if there are innovative lessons from divergent churches that could be applied to your setting that do not require a revolution.

Some of you have been thinking that you'd like to be part of a new kind of faith community, an assembly that doesn't yet exist; one that would be an innovation, something like the divergent churches we've described. So the subject of your attention would concern the essential steps to consider.

One thing we want you to know, and we can't stress this enough, is that *your attention should be on the practices described in this book and how they would take shape in your setting.* In other words, we do not think the way to innovate in an established congregation or to create a divergent church is to start a dinner church because that worked for Simple Church. We do not think you move ahead by finding an outdoor sanctuary with space for a garden, thus duplicating The Garden Church. Do not search the Internet for the closest trail ride business and propose initiating a Cowboy Church in your area.

The way ahead is through careful consideration of what creates religious meaning for your community (whether new or established) and how you will express that meaning through the practices described in this book.

So instead of thinking that you need to start a dinner church because that is what Simple Church does, begin by exploring the activities of breaking bread together that are most congruent with your context. That might mean hosting dinner with every worship service (or it might not). In the churches we studied this particular practice included baking and selling bread, having breakfast together, eating with people who represent different economic realities, raising produce, communion services, and much more. The meaning-making develops because there is something inherently spiritual about sitting down at a table together; whether that means you become a dinner church or not is not the point. The point is that this practice involves a universal human activity that, in the churches we examined, is part of people's search for the Divine. So how would that be true or not true for your congregation?

Your congregation, or the dream you have for a yet-to-be-established congregation, might include immersion in artistic expression. This is true for Convergence Church. Your faith community may or may not benefit from having a theatre group. That was an interest developed naturally from Lisa Cole Smith, the friends she knows, and the city in which she serves. Instead, think through what artistic gifts are natural to you and the neighbors and strangers you see in your neighborhood. How do these visible gifts amount to something more than a new church program, but constitute something about a way of life? Are there painters nearby? Or are there community musicians in close proximity? Identify the forms of art and craft that are native to your location, as Edwin Lacy did with the Wild Goose Christian Community. Don't start a theatre group simply because you read and enjoyed the chapter on artistic expression. Discern and then claim the ways creativity and church are linked to a relationship with the Divine in your setting.

Religion cannot be franchised. When you go to Starbucks—and there are about thirteen thousand such coffee shops in the United States—you experience the essential elements as the same regardless of your location. How you order, the design of the cups, the taste of the mocha, the aroma of coffee, the lighting, the music playing, the placement of the tip jar, and so forth. You expect the experience to be the same.

As you consider what divergent actions to take with your faith community, please do not try to replicate the specific activities of the congregations in this book, or view them as replicable "best practices." When Edwin Lacy began Wild Goose Christian Community in Appalachia, he started with square dancing. That wouldn't make sense if you intend to start a congregation in urban Miami. The takeaway is that Edwin and the folks at Wild Goose are totally at home in the Appalachian culture. They are trying to find out what the Gospel looks like with Appalachian attire. Edwin leads an assembly that uses native symbols and native activities, assimilating them into the religious experience.

Our exploration of divergent churches has shown us that alternative faith communities cannot be created by replication. Rather than transferring the models, strategies, and tactics that have worked elsewhere, you will want to deeply explore what the practices look like in *your* place, among *your* people.

Furthermore, and this is in addition to our observation that religion cannot be franchised, you will want to manage the tension between some orthodoxies of Christendom that developed out of specific, historic contexts and the authentic, religious experiences of your constituents. Remember from chapter 8 how Jonathan of Church at the Square experienced something like the sacrament of communion as he shared the convenience store pizza with his homeless friend.

What if this is communion in a divergent church?

We heard a story, told in a seminary New Testament class, of a woman who had just experienced a Christian conversion. She was enraptured by her newfound faith, and she wanted to be baptized, but she had not yet found a church home. So she baptized herself in a backyard pool. It was a moment of spiritual ecstasy, and her conversion was complete. Many church leaders (including the professor that day) would discount this "baptism" and consider it invalid.

On one hand this is understandable because the professor and those in the tradition he represents are committed to a proper understanding of the sacraments. The integrity, the wholeness, of an important religious commitment is at stake.

On the other hand, in divergent churches it is not only the shape of the community that diverges. We believe the actual religious experience diverges from established, accepted occurrences. If baptism is an outward sign of the inward reality of dying and rising with Christ, and if baptism for adults signifies changes in commitments and changes in the way a person engages the world, then *baptism* is exactly what happened to that woman in the swimming pool. It wasn't by magic of the chlorine water. It was an outward expression of faith representing something that already happened.

What if this is baptism in a divergent church?

The stories of these divergent churches serve as an invitation to consider essential religious practices in a highly contextual manner.

The stories also serve as an invitation to consider essential religious beliefs in distinctive if not peculiar ways. We have found that new forms of congregating also reveal new constructs of faith. The churches of today, divergent or otherwise, are being called to explore the tension between orthodoxy and deviation from orthodoxy.

People are having transformative experiences. Why would we say that a person's transformative experience is not credible because it is not conventional—it doesn't look like it is "supposed" to? Her self-baptism. His 7-Eleven pizza. These are sacred acts and examples of how people are living out their faith.

Many of us are still living out our faith in conventional, suburban mainline congregations; we thank God for such faithful churches. At the same time, new alternative communities are rising up, rooted in Christian tradition but open to the great expanse of human experience with God, and holding on lightly to notions about "correctness" regarding church and faith.

The presence of divergent churches is a summons to loosen up. Permission to experiment is welcomed with greater openness in other arenas than it is in the religious sphere. School systems are trying new types of schools. Medical centers are experimenting with new forms of hospitals. Corporations take risks in ways that churches would never dream about. Most leaders in business, technology, and other sectors of society seem to have a natural tendency toward positive thinking about trial and error, research and development; most of us religious types do not.

People are tinkering with innovation in other sectors not because any single innovation represents an absolute right or wrong, but because of *the human impulse to figure out something new.*

That's one reason for our gratitude toward the divergent church. Blessedly, somebody is willing to try something new. The divergent church leaders we've met are sticking their necks out, running the risk of being called heretical, or being barred from ordination because they can't/won't confess certain tenets. They are risking the very form and concept of church itself. And they are doing so because they believe in God, they seek transcendence, and they long for community. There's not a whole lot in it for them in terms of worldly success. What is at stake for these new leaders? What makes it worth the risk? It is living a life of meaning, a life that *is* an encounter with the Divine. Such a risk, such an encounter is as vital as anything else that we might try to figure out as a human species.

NOTES

1. Innovation

1. Paul Tillich, *Dynamics of Faith* (New York: Harper One, 2001), 1–2.

2. L. Gregory Jones, *Christian Social Innovation: Renewing Wesleyan Witness* (Nashville: Abingdon Press, 2016), 2.

3. Clayton Christensen, Michael Raynor, and Rory McDonald, "What Is Disruptive Innovation?" *Harvard Business Review*, December 19, 2016, accessed April 3, 2017, https://hbr.org/2015/12/what-is-disruptive-innovation.

4. Jones, *Christian Social Innovation*, 2.

5. Thanks to the Rev. Dr. Felicia LaBoy, former associate dean of Black Church Studies at Louisville Presbyterian Theological Seminary for teaching us about the innovation of African-American congregations. She serves St. John's United Methodist Church in Oak Park, Illinois.

6. Richard Pascale, Jerry Sternin, and Monique Sternin, *The Power of Positive Deviance: How Unlikely Innovators Solve the World's Toughest Problems* (Boston: Harvard Business Press, 2010).

7. Tillich, *Dynamics of Faith*, 1.

2. What Constitutes a Church?

1. United States Internal Revenue Service, *Tax Guide for Churches & Religious Organizations* (Washington D.C., 2015), introduction, accessed April 12, 2017, https://www.irs.gov/pub/irs-pdf/p1828.pdf.

2. Ibid., 2.

3. "'Churches' Defined," accessed April 12, 2017, https://www.irs.gov/charities
-non-profits/churches-religious-organizations/churches-defined.

4. Mark Chaves, *Congregations in America* (Cambridge, MA: Harvard University
Press, 2004), 1.

5. Ibid., 1–2.

6. William J. Abraham and James E. Kirby, *The Oxford Handbook of Methodist
Studies* (Oxford: Oxford University Press, 2011), 368.

7. Gordon Lathrop, *Holy People: A Liturgical Ecclesiology* (Minneapolis, MN:
Fortress Press, 2007), 1–4.

8. Ibid., 5.

9. Angie Thurston and Casper ter Kuile, "How We Gather," April 2015, accessed
April 4, 2017, www.howwegather.org.

10. Ibid., 8.

11. Ibid., 19.

12. National Congregations Study, 2012, accessed April 20, 2017, http://www
.thearda.com/ConQS/qs_295.asp.

3. Practices

1. In 1664, Samuel Crossman wrote the words. In 1918, John Ireland composed
the tune, "Love Unknown."

2. Alasdair C. MacIntyre, *After Virtue: A Study in Moral Theory* (Notre Dame,
IN: University of Notre Dame Press, 2012), 187.

3. Dorothy Bass and Craig Dykstra, "Times of Yearning, Practices of Faith," in
Practicing Our Faith: A Way of Life for a Searching People (San Francisco: Jossey-Bass,
2010), 5.

4. Lillian Daniel, *When Spiritual but Not Religious Is Not Enough: Seeing God in
Surprising Places, Even the Church* (New York: Jericho Books, 2013).

5. Root and Branch Church, "At Root and Branch We Are Growing," accessed March 20, 2017, http://www.rootandbranchchurch.org/the-church/.

6. Marianne Sawicki, *Seeing the Lord: Resurrection and Early Christian Practices* (Minneapolis, MN: Fortress Press, 1994), 79.

7. Doug Hanner is not only the clergy leader of a divergent church, he is a colleague of ours (the authors) at the Center for Congregations.

8. Pierre Bourdieu, *The Logic of Practice* (Stanford, CA: Stanford University Press, 1974), 52.

9. Ibid. 55.

4. The Practice of Shaping Community

1. "Galileo Church," accessed July 31, 2017, http://galileochurch.org/.

2. "Our Biggest Deals," accessed July 31, 2017, http://galileochurch.org/our-biggest-deals/.

3. Dietrich Bonhoeffer, *Letters and Papers from Prison* (New York: Touchstone, 1997), 370.

4. John Dominic Crossan, *Jesus: A Revolutionary Biography* (New York: Harper-One, 2009), 74–75.

5. "Historic Campus Architecture Project," accessed July 31, 2017, http://hcap.artstor.org/cgi-bin/library?a=d&d=p964.

6. Eugene H. Peterson, *Subversive Spirituality* (Grand Rapids: W. B. Eerdmans, 2000), 239.

7. Galileo Church Pastoral Staff, Missional Logistics Team, Care and Feeding Team, *Litany of Confession and Absolution*, March 19, 2017.

8. Bonhoeffer, *Letters and Papers from Prison*, 7.

5. The Practice of Conversation

1. From conversation with Gil Rendle on various occasions in consultation with the Indianapolis Center for Congregations.

2. "Spirituality," Valley and Mountain Church, accessed May 17, 2017, https://valleyandmountain.org/spirituality.

3. John S. McClure, *The Roundtable Pulpit: Where Leadership and Preaching Meet* (Nashville: Abingdon Press, 1995), 1–16.

4. "Root and Branch Church," accessed April 28, 2017, http://www.rootand branchchurch.org/the-church/.

5. "About," Root and Branch Church, accessed April 30, 2017, https://www .facebook.com/pg/rootandbranchchurch/about/.

6. "Simple Church," accessed May 2, 2017, http://www.simpleumc.org/.

7. Anne Tyler, *Saint Maybe* (New York: Knopf, 1991), 118.

8. Deborah Tannen, *That's Not What I Meant! How Conversational Style Makes or Breaks Relationships*, reprint edition (New York: William Morrow, 2011), 34.

9. The ground rules are from a Welcome Table liturgy developed by Root and Branch.

10. Daniel J. Siegel, *Mindsight: The New Science of Personal Transformation* (New York: Bantam Books, 2010), 61.

11. John Caputo and Gary Gutting, "Deconstructing God," *New York Times*, March 9, 2014, accessed June 1, 2017, https://opinionator.blogs.nytimes .com/2014/03/09/deconstructing-god/?mcubz=2,.

12. Ibid.

13. Frederick Buechner, *Telling Secrets* (HarperCollins: New York, 1991), 82.

14. Ibid., 93.

6. The Practice of Artistic Expression

1. "Convergence," accessed May 24, 2017, www.ourconvergence.org.

2. "Singing Our Lives," accessed June 22, 2017, http://www.practicingourfaith .org/singing-our-lives.

3. Debrorah Haynes, *The Vocation of the Artist* (Cambridge, MA: Cambridge University Press, 1997), 4–5.

4. Si Kahn, "Gone Gonna Rise Again," 1975.

7. The Practice of Breaking Bread

1. "Moments That Shimmer," accessed June 1, 2017, https://gardenchurchsp .org/moments-shimmer-rev-anna-woofenden-2-26-2017/.

2. Ibid.

3. "Why Eating the Same Food Increases People's Trust and Cooperation," ac- cessed July 29, 2017, http://www.npr.org/2017/02/02/512998465/why-eating-the -same-food-increases-peoples-trust-and-cooperation.

8. The Practice of Community Engagement

1. Robert D. Lupton, *Toxic Charity: How Churches and Charities Hurt Those They Help (and How to Reverse It)* (New York: HarperOne, 2011), 6–7.

2. "Rick Telander: A Season under the Gun," *Chicago Sun Times*, Febru- ary 22, 2017, accessed June 7, 2017, http://www.suntimeshighschoolsports .com/2017/02/22/rick-telander-season-gun/.

3. "About Us," The Community Church, accessed July 29, 2017, http://www .thecommunitychurch.us/a-bit-about-us.html.

4. The first time we heard such a distinction was from the Rev. Mike Mather, pastor of Broadway United Methodist Church in Indianapolis, Indiana.

5. Richard Pascale, Jerry Sternin, and Monique Sternin, *The Power of Positive Deviance: How Unlikely Innovators Solve the World's Toughest Problems* (Cambridge, MA: Harvard Business Press, 2010), 3–7.

9. The Practice of Hospitality

1. Toni Morrison, *Beloved* (New York: Vintage, 2010), 6.

2. http://www.script-o-rama.com/movie_scripts/l/little-man-tate-script-transcript .html.

3. David G. Buttrick, *Speaking Parables: A Homiletic Guide* (Louisville, KY: Westminster John Knox Press, 2000), 183–85.

4. https://gardenchurchsp.org/moments-shimmer-rev-anna-woofenden-2-26 -2017/.

5. Ibid.

6. Ibid.

7. Ibid.

BIBLIOGRAPHY

Abraham, William J., and James E. Kirby. *The Oxford Handbook of Methodist Studies*. Oxford: Oxford University Press, 2011.

Bass, Dorothy C., ed. *Practicing Our Faith: A Way of Life for a Searching People*. 2nd ed. John Wiley & Sons, 2010.

Bonhoeffer, Dietrich. *Letters and Papers from Prison*. New York: Touchstone, 1997.

Buttrick, David G. *Speaking Parables: A Homiletic Guide*. Louisville, KY: Westminster John Knox Press, 2000.

Chaves, Mark. *Congregations in America*. Cambridge, MA: Harvard University Press, 2004.

Christiensen, Clayton, Michael Raynor, and Rory McDonald. "What Is Disruptive Innovation?" *Harvard Business Review*. December 19, 2016. Accessed July 10, 2017. https://hbr.org/2015/12/what-is-disruptive-innovation.

"'Churches' Defined." Accessed April 12, 2017. https://www.irs.gov/charities-non-profits/churches-religious-organizations/churches-defined.

Crossan, John Dominic. *Jesus: A Revolutionary Biography*. New York: HarperOne, 2009.

Jones, L. Gregory. *Christian Social Innovation: Renewing Wesleyan Witness*. Nashville: Abingdon Press, 2016.

Lathrop, Gordon. *Holy People: A Liturgical Ecclesiology*. Minneapolis, MN: Fortress Press, 2007.

Lupton, Robert D. *Toxic Charity: How Churches and Charities Hurt Those They Help (and How to Reverse It)*. New York: HarperOne, 2011.

MacIntyre, Alasdair C. *After Virtue: A Study in Moral Theory*. 3rd ed. Notre Dame, IN: University of Notre Dame Press, 2012.

Morrison, Toni. *Beloved*. New York: Vintage, 2010.

Pascale, Richard, Jerry Sternin, and Monique Sternin. *The Power of Positive Deviance: How Unlikely Innovators Solve the World's Toughest Problems*. Boston: Harvard Business Press, 2010.

Peterson, Eugene H. *Subversive Spirituality*. Grand Rapids: W. B. Eerdmans, 2000.

Siegel, Daniel J. *Mindsight: The New Science of Personal Transformation*. New York: Bantam Books, 2010.

Tannen, Deborah. *That's Not What I Meant! How Conversational Style Makes or Breaks Relationships*. Reprint ed. New York: William Morrow, 2011.

ter Kuile, Casper, and Angie Thurston. "How We Gather." April 2015. Accessed April 4, 2017. www.howwegather.org.

Tillich, Paul. *Dynamics of Faith*. New York: Perennial, 2001.

Tyler, Anne. *Saint Maybe*. New York: Knopf, 1991.

United States Internal Revenue Service. *Tax Guide for Churches and Religious Organizations*. 2015.